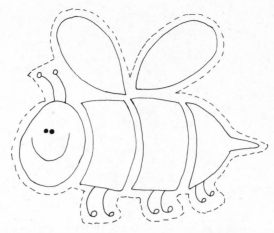

QUILTING
& Patchwork

By the Editors of Sunset Books

LANE BOOKS · MENLO PARK, CALIFORNIA

Acknowledgments

Since the very beginning, quilting and patchwork have been far removed from the closed, competitive world of the arts. Their real essence lies in an unselfish sharing of new ideas for the artistic beautification of practical items, something that is not very common among artists and craftsmen today. The creative strength of generations of men and women are proclaimed by the stunning beauty of the thousands of old and new quilts we see around us, many of which are the results of years of loving work.

Quiltmaking today hasn't abandoned any of these wonderful qualities. Without exception, quiltmakers from local quilting circles to the best nationally known designers and writers have responded with unselfish generosity when contacted in regard to this book, willingly sharing their information and ideas.

Very, very special thanks to Donna Renshaw and Belva Long, who were the most generous of all in the sharing of ideas, time and unlimited patience. They truly exemplified the spirit of quiltmaking. Thanks, too, to the following people, without whose help this book could not have been accomplished: Nancy Cahners, Pat Curto, Ruth Garbett, Doris Hoover, Doris Hubner, Elsie Jensen, Vicki Johnson, Sue Koster, Mrs. Henry Kiyomura, Jean Ray Laury, Lorena Lentz, K. Lee Manuel, Margaret E. Mersman, Anne Mitchell, Betty Patterson, Judy Raffael, Ruth Roller, Shirley Sferra, Cleo Vlught, the many women who took time to answer our questionnaire, and the museums and art galleries who have been so helpful.

Edited by Alyson Smith Gonsalves

Special Consultant: Donna Renshaw

Design: John Flack

Drawings: Marsha Kline

Cover: Ohio Star Tote Bag (page 47), designed by Alyson Smith Gonsalves, made by Anne Mitchell.
Photographer: Lars Speyer

Executive Editor, Sunset Books, David E. Clark

Design Credits: Gheen Abbott III, courtesy Grace Larsen, 74 right; **Kay Alexander,** 76 upper left; **Karen Bakke,** 77 lower right; **Charles Counts and the Rising Fawn Quilters,** 77 upper left; **Courtesy Daughters of Utah Pioneers,** 4, 5, 7 upper left; **Jessica Dvorak,** 78 upper left; **Pine Eisfeller,** 68 bottom; **Alyson Smith Gonsalves,** 34 (quilt), 36, 39, 42 right, 44, 47 (purse), 50 all, 52 upper right, lower left and right; **Doris Hoover,** 79 upper right; **Elsie P. Jensen,** 66 bottom; **Mrs. Henry Kiyomura,** 37; **Marsha Kline,** 39; **Sue Koster,** 42 left; **Mark Law,** 77 lower left; **Joan Lintault,** 75 upper right; **Belva Long,** 76 upper right, 79 upper left; **K. Lee Manuel, Doris Hubner,** 77 upper right; **Kathryn McCardle,** 78 lower left; **Maxine McClendon,** 75 lower right; **Nancy McComb,** 75 upper left; **Courtesy of M. H. deYoung Memorial Museum, San Francisco,** 7 upper and lower right; **Anne Mitchell,** 47 (tie); **"Four Quilts by Judy Raffael and Friends,"** 79 lower right; **Bets Ramsey,** 78 upper right; **Donna Renshaw,** 45, 52 upper left, 61, 63, 66 top, 68 top and bottom; **Anne M. Scholten,** 75 lower left; **J. H. Koslan Schwartz,** 78 lower right; **Courtesy of Shelbourne Museum Inc., Shelbourne, Vermont,** 74 left, 79 lower left; **Georgiana Spencer,** 76 lower left; **Midge Stark,** 76 lower right.

Tenth Printing November 1976

Contents

It's Fun to Make It Yourself

A Colorful Array of Quilting and Patchwork

A Gallery of Quilts

Special Features:

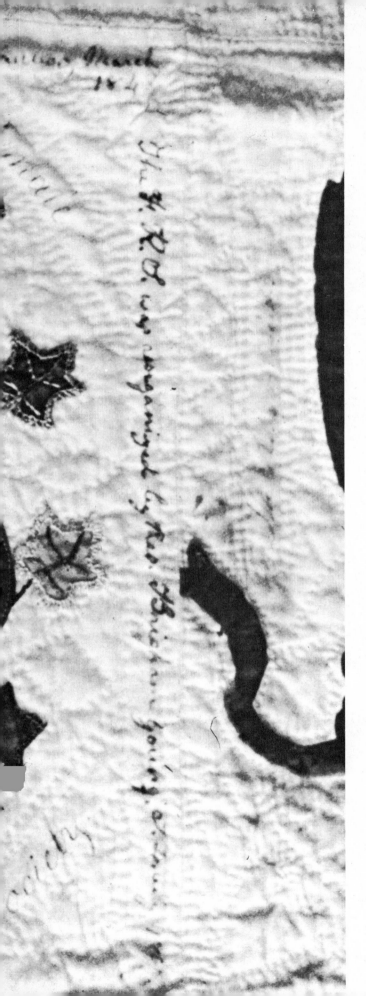

It's Fun to Make It Yourself

What are contemporary, colorful, traditional, ecological, inexpensive, and fun all at the same time? If you haven't guessed by now—quilting and patchwork.

Basically, they're both techniques. The final results may range from a king-sized bedcover to a beanbag, but the paths from each idea to each completed item follow approximately the same steps, and once you've mastered the methods, the door lies open to a whole new appreciation of and involvement with fabric. When you discover for yourself what effects stitching, filling, and piecing can create, you'll look at everything through new eyes. It's true—almost anything can be made or decorated using these techniques.

The results can be practical or artistic, simple or involved. It all depends on the desire of the individual to give it a try. There are no absolute rules—bend them a little; there are no absolute designs—create your own schemes in line and color. There are also no age barriers. Here is something for the smallest child to the oldest senior citizen: beautiful color, useful work, and something created with love and enjoyment to last a long time. One lasting creation, a beautiful hand-embroidered and appliqued Friendship Quilt, is shown on page 7 (details at left and below).

History in the Making

*The history of quilting and patchwork is a fascinating evolution of these
techniques from their simple beginnings long ago to their incredibly varied use
today. Take a trip through time and follow quilting and patchwork
as they evolve from their Far Eastern beginnings to become an American tradition.*

Quilting could be Chinese in origin, or Egyptian; perhaps it began somewhere in the cities or countrysides of Persia or India. However long ago it did begin, one thing is certain — quilting was born of necessity. The bitter cold of winter and the chill wetness of the rainy season made warmth literally a matter of life or death.

Discovered in the Holy Land, quilting rode across the Mediterranean into Europe beneath the heavy armor of battle-weary Crusaders. The realization that such padding protected their bodies from the cold as well as from chafing must have planted the idea of quilted clothing and bedcovers in the minds of Europeans. In any case, the introduction of armor padding into Northern Europe in the 12th century marked the beginning of quilting as we know it today.

The making of padded materials for warmth was greatly accelerated by a drastic climatic change in Western Europe during the 14th century. Suddenly the land was gripped by devastating winters, the coldest in the memory of man. Great rivers froze and the land was covered with snow. During these years, the quilted bedcover was firmly established as a necessity; quilting frames were created, and special tools for joining layers of fabric were devised. The women used anything they could find for filling — lamb's wool, moss, feathers, and even grass were sewn into quilts for added warmth.

Initially simple in execution, quilting stitches eventually became more elaborate and decorative. Scrolls, ornamental motifs, and applique were common decorations, not only on bedding but also on such articles of clothing as shoes, gloves, and caps.

In the countries of Southern Europe, where winters were less severe, quilting was regarded as a means of embellishment rather than a necessity. Ecclesiastical garments, heavy silks, and velvets were enhanced by intricate stitches. The beginnings of *trapunto,* or Italian Quilting, can be found in the Sicilian cable stitch, used to highlight a design by inserting a cord between two stitched layers of fabric.

The art of quilting was spread to a great extent by the intermarriage of European royal families. New ideas and techniques arrived with many a noble bride-to-be and were quickly adapted to the current taste.

Though primarily used for superfluous decoration in the South of Europe, quilting became so necessary in the North as a means of protection against the weather that quiltmaking evolved into a sort of cottage industry in Britain and Holland. Quilts, or bed furniture, as they were called, rose to such levels of artistry and craftsmanship that, upon the death of their owners, they were bequeathed to deserving relatives as prized possessions. These coveted articles were often embroidered with mottoes sternly reminding those who slept beneath of the frailty of human character. The appearance of these early quilts was quite different from the gay, sometimes antic look of the American quilt. They were generally whole pieces of cloth intricately quilted with an overall design. Sometimes they would contain applique work or embroidery as the principle decoration, but they were all alike in that the material for the quilt top was a single piece of fabric.

Many customs and superstitions grew from the practice of quilting, influencing the lives of the young girls, wives, and mothers who spent hours seated at the quilting frame. They began at a tender age to produce quilts of increasing complexity, all aiming for a full dowry chest on the eve of their marriage. The last and most beautiful, the Bridal Quilt, was not begun until the young woman was formally engaged, as to begin before this moment was to invite bad fortune. Friends and relatives were invited over to help finish the marriage quilt, a good excuse for showing off a hand-sewn trousseau.

This custom, along with many others, emigrated from the Old World to the New. Each pilgrim family departing the shores of Europe had in their possession complete sets of bed furniture in preparation for the hardships ahead. And there were many.

Uninformed and ill-prepared, these men and women struggled through terrible winters and bone-wearying labor to build new lives for themselves. So poor were the settlers and so isolated from European conveniences that everything was re-used and re-used again, including quilts. When worn, they were repaired with scraps of old clothing, gradually acquiring the appearance of a patchworked top. Those tops were certainly not as beautiful as the patchwork tops that we know, for the materials used by the pilgrims were "sad colors," sturdy dark reds, blues, and browns.

One might think that these patched and worn covers marked a low point in the history of quilting, but the

Exquisite example *of hand embroidery and applique, this friendship quilt was completed over 100 years ago.*

Silk pelisse *made between 1800 and 1810 shows quilted trim on cuffs and along front closure.*

opposite is true. They were the beginnings of the beautiful piecework patterns of the 1700s and 1800s, designs of arresting originality which chronicled the history of the settling of North America.

Eventually, the Eastern coast of the Americas was settled. Shipping lines carrying goods for the settlers were established, making it possible for the seaboard housewife to obtain precious bolts of imported cloth. She was more fortunate than her inland sister, who depended on her own hard work to spin, dye, and weave flax or wool into usable lengths of fabric. At this time patchwork first established itself as a useful technique for the preparation of bed covers, prompting tentative attempts at making pleasing color arrangements.

In the southern United States, as in the south of Europe, covers were quilted for decoration and made of beautiful fabrics, chosen not for durability but for beauty. Records exist which catalogue these exquisite coverlets for estate sale, in wills, and in marriage agreements.

For many people, the settling of the Eastern seaboard brought feelings of restlessness and a desire for open space. This desire carried pioneers westward for many years and, again, quilts went with them. Exposure to new land and new experiences began to create new ideas in the minds of pioneer women. Patchwork tops became opportunities to display their feelings and concepts of America, the happiness, the trials, and the uncertainty of frontier life. Cherished garments found their way into the quilt top after years of service, and, preserved in this manner, the personal history of a family could be traced from the oldest to the newest patch.

Quilts indeed became chronicles of a way of life, but they also left an impression on the structure of our social life. Quilting bees grew to be great social events, marking anything from a betrothal party to a way to pass a cold winter's day in the company of friends. In the evening, after the last stitch was taken and the frame put away, the men would appear and a rousing good-natured evening would begin.

Eventually American cloth production reached the point where fabric could be produced in many colors and more cheaply than the materials carried by boat from Europe. At about the same time, applique work grew in popularity. This practice of laying one fabric over another for design was frowned upon by the original settlers, who considered it a flagrant waste of precious cloth. Now, thanks to the inexpensive cloth produced by American looms, applique was welcomed as a new way to embellish those quilts reserved for special occasions. Such quilts were carefully stored and only occasionally brought out, accounting for the great number of appliqued pieces shown in museums today. Patchwork bedcovers, however, were put to daily use. Few remain for us to see after years of constant wear and tear.

Quilt-making continued to be a popular home art until the advent of machine-made goods marked the end of quilting as a common household activity. For several decades quilting and patchwork were sporadically resumed and just as sporadically ignored until, during the 1960s, quilt-making, along with other handcrafts, was recognized for its unique qualities and revived. A certain dissatisfaction with mass-produced items seems to have triggered a new desire for the originality and freshness of hand-made articles. Today, quiltmaking and patchwork are practiced by housewife and artist alike, both appreciative of the techniques, qualities, and heritage inherent in the patchwork quilt.

Harvest Sun, *an unusual design, is dramatically displayed in this cream, maroon, and deep green quilt made in South Carolina and dating from about 1850.*

General Techniques

This section of the book will help you to understand which tools and materials are needed for quilting and patchwork and how they are used. Knowing this information will make it possible for you to enjoy working in these media without the frustration of trying to cope with unfamiliar techniques.

The first "rule" to follow is: relax! Rome wasn't built in one day, and neither was a quilt. Take your time, enjoy the experience, and avoid any fears of restrictive do's and don'ts. Eventually, experience will teach you what can and what cannot be done, but in the meantime here are some helpful hints to make working in a new medium as troublefree as possible.

The following pages of this section carry information on materials, equipment, planning, and general methods used in creating quilted and patchworked items. The subjects covered here are basic to all techniques discussed in this book and should come in handy anywhere. A glossary can be found on page 80 for use in clarifying the meanings of common terms.

Equipment

Times may have changed since the first American quilts were made back in the 17th century, but there's one thing that hasn't: a basic list of quilt-making tools.

The most basic of basics are needles, thread, pins, and scissors.

Needles. For sewing and quilting, a No. 7 — No. 10 "between" needle is preferred for making small, even stitches. A milliners' No. 3 — No. 9 needle is long and sharp, very useful for applique work. Although a variety of needles may be used, these are suggested for their special modifications.

Thread. Though quilting thread, a strong, almost stiff filament, is the best material for actual quilting, it is not easy to find and comes in only a limited color range. Mail-order craft catalogues and some specialty stores may carry it. Many quilters have found that the newly-developed polyester core-wrapped thread made for sewing knitted fabrics has the stretch and color selection they desire. It does have a tendency to knot up and fray at the eye of the needle, a condition that can be avoided by knotting or anchoring the thread end that is cut from the spool. This technique will also work for other types of thread. Heavy-duty threads are especially good to work with because of their strength and durability. Be sure to purchase fresh, new thread, for older thread may have rotted and weakened.

Pins. Glass-headed pins are desirable for general use. Small and sharp, they are perfect for pinning accurate seams and for anchoring one layer of fabric to another. They come in two sizes and are easy to see and to remove.

Scissors. Lay your pinking shears aside; they aren't generally used in cutting these kinds of patterns. A sharp shears with good points will serve you well, and small embroidery scissors will also come in handy for tiny snips and for clipping curves in applique pieces.

The following useful tools are important aids in making patterns and tracings and for fine, accurate work with fabrics; they may be found in office or art supply stores.

Yardstick, ruler and tape measure. These three items are necessary for measuring surfaces to be covered, laying out yardage, and tracing and making patterns for quilting, patchwork, or applique.

Quilting necessities *include thread (quilting, heavy duty, and polyester), needles, shears, and embroidery scissors.*

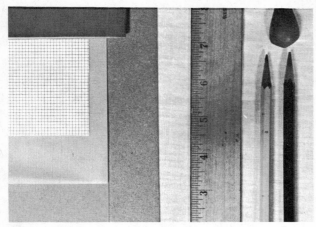

Helpful tools: *dressmaker's carbon, stiff plastic, hard and soft lead pencils, a small balloon, cardboard, and graph and tissue papers for making your patterns.*

Suitable fabrics *for quilting and patchwork would include (left to right) broadcloth, calico, cotton, flannel, gingham, muslin, satin, velvet, wool, and knit fabrics.*

Semi-hard pencil. Use either a 6B architect's pencil or a blue-lead pencil for tracing patterns and for marking seams. Be sure the points are sharp for the sake of accuracy. Soft lead pencils will smudge your fabric and come off on your hands. A gum eraser will remove most pencil marks and a pastry brush will whisk away the eraser rubbings.

Tracing paper. These thin tissue-like sheets are necessary for copying patterns and making corrections.

Graph paper. A handy tool for creating new designs or for establishing real accuracy in old ones. Isometric graph papers are ideal for diamond-shaped motifs (their grid lines run at acute angles with one another).

Paper. For quilting patterns, rolls of newsprint (not newspaper—the ink will mar your fabric), shelf paper, or butcher paper can give the length needed for designing or laying out long quilting motifs. If you can't find any of these, just tape sheets of paper together by putting tape on their backs to make a continuous roll.

Plastic, cardboard, or sandpaper sheets. These are materials for making your templates, or patterns. Cardboard is traditionally used for patterns, with sandpaper following a close second because of its ability to grip fabrics firmly. You can expect both cardboard and sandpaper to wear down around the edges eventually, robbing patterns of any accuracy. Taped edges can hold off the deterioration for awhile, but the real solution lies in the use of a firm, tough material in its place. Resourceful quilters of the past often had a favorite pattern cut from tin by the local blacksmith. Since there aren't too many of these fellows left today, a more modern and practical solution is the use of plastic. It can come from old bleach bottles, distilled water containers, or in sheet form from the local plastics supply store. Plastic is one material that will not wear down, is flexible, transparent, easy to cut, and inexpensive.

Dressmaker's carbon. Using dressmaker's carbon, you can easily copy patterns onto another surface with a tracing wheel. Transfer pencils are quick and very accurate, as you can draw right over your pencil drawing and iron the design onto any desired surface.

Iron and ironing board. For preparing applique pieces and for creasing down a seam, happiness is a warm iron. Keep one close by for quick basting, turning of seams, and for ironing out wrinkles.

The following accessories are helpful but optional:

Thimble. Small but strategic, a thimble is very handy for preventing sore fingers. Make sure you use one that fits your index finger properly.

Rubber balloon. That's right. Strange as it may seem, a piece of balloon wrapped around a stubborn needle will greatly help in pulling it out of heavy or thick fabric.

Wax. Beeswax, paraffin, or even a candle are useful for strengthening thread, making it slick and easy to pull through fabric.

Quilting frame or hoop. This item, once a household fixture, can be considered optional for all but the most intricate and difficult quilts. The inexpensive construction and use of a sturdy, home-made frame is discussed in the section on quilting.

Fabrics and fillers

One way to make quilting easy and fun is to choose and use the proper materials. Certain types of fabrics are more suitable than others for being cut into patches and applique pieces, and for being stitched into beautiful designs.

Fabrics for surface decoration or for piecing should be smooth, soft, non-raveling and colorfast, with a firm weave. If they aren't pre-shrunk, they should be washed, which will also remove any sizing present. (Sizing can make sewing difficult, especially in handwork.) These fabrics are very good for piecing or quilting: broadcloth, calico, cotton, cotton satin, flannel, gingham, muslin, satin, silk, velvet, velveteen, wool, and the newer knit fabrics.

Inexpensive muslin sheeting, flannel, or challis make for a sturdy backing; so do any of the materials mentioned for use in piecing or quilting if the piece is to be reversible. Hard to penetrate with a needle, permapress, percales, expensive heavy satins, and stiff materials should definitely be avoided. Loosely woven cloth, as well as transparent fabric, are not good choices either, because they ravel and wear out quickly. However, for the sake of artistic creativity, these different kinds of cloth — if chosen with discretion — can be used to good effect in certain types of fabric construction. Items receiving hard wear and constant use should contain the same types of sturdy cloth. Imagine what would happen in a washing machine to a delicate square of voile flanked by tough corduroy. (In fact, quilts or other such handmade items dear to your heart should be dry-cleaned.)

Try to use only material of good quality; it will pay off in the long run. Inexpensive, poorly-made fabrics can shrink, wrinkle, wear out, and bleed dye when washed, obliterating in seconds all of the care lavished on a finished piece. Good material can come from sewing scraps, portions of old clothing, or directly off the bolt. Be sure to test it first for shrinkage, dye-fastness, and wrinkling. To set dye in a questionable piece of material, add ⅓ cup of vinegar to 1 gallon of boiling water, then soak the cloth for several minutes. Another important point: be sure to buy enough of each color, as dye lots vary and you may have trouble matching a color later on.

Filler or stuffing can run from the ridiculous to the sublime. When times were hard, such things as newspapers, cornhusks, and rags were used. Today, the quilter has access to a great variety of filler in many types, sizes, and materials.

HANDS ACROSS THE FRAME: THE FRIENDSHIP QUILT

Few things are more personal yet practical than quilts. For this reason, many early American women thought of quilts as fine gifts and gave them often. Since each person usually went her own way in designing her block, friendship quilts were offerings from the heart rather than artistic masterpieces because of the dizzying conglomeration that resulted when all blocks were sewn together. If a basic color scheme and design concept had previously been agreed upon, the quilt could be exceptionally beautiful.

Many of these quilts were intended to be tangible memories. As families moved West, a friendship quilt became a treasured reminder of homes left behind. Sometimes each block was signed by its maker, then embroidered so the signature would last.

At times, individual blocks were exchanged between friends. On other occasions, ladies presented their work at a formal gathering to the person being honored. Often girls would make a friendship quilt for an engaged friend as a wedding present. Later the giving of individual blocks became common, a practice that might have led to engagement parties and presents as we know them.

Friendship quilts can be personalized in many ways. The square itself is, of course, the product of a friend's skill and can include her signature, a brief note, or a favorite recipe. Possibilities are endless.

Because friendship quilts were cared for meticulously and used only occasionally, many examples exist today. Obviously, they were highly prized.

Cotton batting is the traditional filler for American quilts. Though it's been used a long time, it has several serious drawbacks. There is a tendency to lump when washed, thick and thin spots appear in the batt, and it is not very fluffy. Because fine, close stitches are necessary to hold the batt in place, only an experienced quilter who desires a completely traditional result should attempt the use of cotton batting.

Old mattress pads, flannel or cotton sheeting, and old blankets are other types of filler which can be used for tied quilts and other items not closely quilted. They hold up well but have no puffiness and can be heavy. Wash to preshrink before using.

The best material available for filler is the dacron batt. Made in many sizes, thicknesses, and weights, it is ideal for quilting. Dacron can be light and fluffy, creating a thick quilt with highly raised areas, or the layers can be pulled apart and thinned for a less puffy look. Some dacron batts contain interlocking fibers to prevent shifting and lumping, and some are coated with a glaze that gives a smooth, stable working surface. Because of its versatility, the dacron batt can be either quilted or tied, allowing for a wide range of applications. It is completely washable and can take tremendous wear.

Choosing color and design

When you get right down to it, every quilted or patchworked piece is an exercise in design and color arrangement. Your ideas can come from a variety of sources, such as design books, advertisements, magazines, nature, or adaptations of a design from another medium, but all are arrangements of the elements of design and the shades of color. To plan ideas more successfully, it helps to have some idea of color and design principles.

Color ideas. One of the most effective carriers of emotion and feeling, color can be relaxing or invigorating, cool or warm, melancholy or gay. Since we all have certain reactions to certain colors, it is a good idea to think seriously about colors in relation to what you are making and where it will be used. Start by asking the recipients of your efforts for their color preferences. Then combine this with knowledge of the room that it will occupy. Period, style, and mood of decor should harmonize for most effective results. Contrasts are also good but more difficult to plan successfully.

The basic colors are red, blue, and yellow. Intermediate colors — created by the mixture of primary colors — include magenta, green, and orange. Tertiary colors appear when adjacent primary and secondary colors are mixed. Such a vast array of shades exists that it will be up to the individual to make a final choice on color. For ideas, notice what colors are used in the photographs and art work you see around you. Try to keep your color arrangements simple at first, but most important, choose colors that you will enjoy working with. To choose color arrangements, it helps to separate fabrics into tonal groups and to make a sample block to check design and color; you may dislike the design once it is made up. A layout plan on ¼-inch graph paper (¼″ = 1″) is helpful too and will give the overall

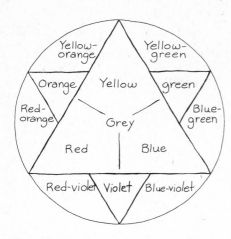

Color wheel is a helpful tool when planning color arrangements. Notice groupings of warm and cool colors.

look of the finished piece. Colored pencils or crayons can be used to plot color designs or layouts.

Planning and sizing designs. The balance and unity of the elements in your work depend on a basic knowledge of design principles. Try to keep the sizes of all units in relationship with one another; unify the elements by connecting them to one another visually; keep your elements balanced with one another by thinking in terms of color, size, and shape of the individual pieces; vary your theme for contrast; and create rhythm in your treatment of lines, spaces, and the relationship of one area to another.

How to enlarge or reduce a design. Patterns are very rarely the exact size you'll need for your projects, so a method for enlarging or decreasing designs is useful. Trace your design onto a sheet of tissue paper marked with a grid pattern of either 1-inch squares or 2-inch squares, depending on the size of the design. On a second sheet of paper, draw a grid pattern containing the same number of squares as the original grid, making the squares larger or smaller, depending on whether you will be reducing or enlarging the design. Transfer the design from each square in the first grid to each corresponding square in the second grid until the entire design is the desired size.

Here are other methods for enlarging or reducing a design: take a slide of the design and project it onto a wall in the desired size; use an opaque projector to enlarge a printed or drawn design; use a pantograph ($4-$14), a mechanical device sold in art supply stores that enlarges your design by tracing over its outline; or take your design to a photocopying service ($3 and up) listed in the yellow pages of the phone book and let them enlarge it to the size you wish.

Enlarging or reducing quilt blocks. Most quilt blocks are based on a square divided into 4, 9, 16, or smaller equal squares. This common trait makes it possible to easily enlarge or reduce any design based on a block. First, look at the design carefully and decide how many squares the block is divided into. Cut a square of

paper the desired size and fold it into the proper number of squares. Using a straight edge and a pencil, copy the design onto the opened paper square, using the fold marks as a placement guide. Some designs are based on triangles, crosses, or diamonds and can be copied by folding and marking your square of paper accordingly. Here's where graph paper can be helpful. If you want minute accuracy, draw your square in the desired size onto a sheet of graph paper and decide what types of units your original design contains. Divide the graphed square into the same type of division and use the intersections of the grid lines to plot a layout of your design.

Designs based on the diamond, hexagon, triangle, or pentagon can be easily plotted on isometric graph paper. This sheet carries a grid made up of diagonally intersecting lines that create the acute angles needed for designs containing sharp points.

The path to perfect planning

It's fun to think about the things you want to make and to plan how they'll look when they're all finished, but not too many people want to think about the mathematics of the situation. Questions like "How big shall it be?" and "How much material will it take?" can frighten you right out of your rosy daydream and turn off your enthusiasm. Though it's hard to know just where to begin, what measurements are necessary, and how to estimate yardage, don't let that stifle your desire to piece and quilt because the following paragraphs will make all calculations easy.

Planning and layout. First, let's take a look at the planning and layout of a successful bedcover. Here are some standard measurements for the length and width of the average bed. A crib-size mattress is 27″ x 48″, twin beds measure 39″ x 75″; doubles are 54″ x 75″; queensize mattresses measure 60″ x 75″; and the kingsize will be 72″ x 84″. Because lengths of beds can vary, it's best to check your bed against the sizes listed and make adjustments accordingly. This will give a basic size for your quilt.

Now decide what type of quilt you wish. Will it be a complete bedspread, a coverlet for cool nights, or a throw for quick naps? This decision will determine the overall finished size.

A *bedspread* requires enough material on three sides to reach the floor or to cover the top of a dust ruffle, so measure from the edge of the bed to the length you desire for the overhang and add this to the sides and the foot of the quilt. Next, you'll want to add 18″ to 20″ to the length of the quilt to cover the pillows. Now add 4″ to 6″ all around to allow for seams and the amount of material taken up when the cover is quilted.

A *coverlet-sized quilt* will be used at night for extra warmth, so there is no need for material to cover the pillow area. You will need a fair amount of overhang on the sides and the foot of the piece to allow for the amount taken up by a sleeping person, so add a few inches all around. Add 4″ to 6″ on all sides for seams and for the amount the piece will "shrink" when quilted.

A *throw* measures approximately 4 feet by 6 feet,

enough to cover the body comfortably for a short period of time. This size is also good for car robes and stadium rugs. Add the customary 4″ to 6″ all around for seams and quilting ease.

Now decide on your basic design. Will you use blocks or an overall motif? Will you have a border? For an overall design, determine where the edges of the design area will fall. You may wish to allow space for a border on the top of the quilt, the sides of the bed, or you may desire no border at all.

If blocks are chosen, decide how large the individual blocks will be and how they will be set together. Blocks are usually between 10″ and 18″ in size and can be joined in several ways. Strips can be placed between the blocks, the blocks may be sewn directly to one another, or plain blocks can be alternated with decorated blocks.

Decide how many and what size blocks fit the width and the length of the bed, and how they will be combined. Perhaps you have a double bed measuring 54″ x 75″ and you decide on 14″ square blocks. Depending on how they will be set together, either 3 or 4 blocks will fit across the bed and 5 will fit the length. This makes a total of either 15 or 20 blocks. A bit of juggling will be necessary to place them to your satisfaction, as the number of blocks chosen and how they are set together will determine whether they overhang the edges of the bed or fall short.

The same basic rules can be applied to other projects. Take overall measurements of the area you want to cover, decide how you will treat the surface decoration, and add a few inches for seams and ease.

Estimating yardage. Judging how much fabric is necessary isn't difficult if you've measured accurately. Most material comes in a standard width of 45″ and even as large as 60″; sheet muslin can be purchased in 72″ widths. The treatment of the surface design will decide how you will figure yardage. If you will be creating an overall quilting design or appliqueing pieces to one large piece of material, then you will need to figure out how many widths will cover the surface of your piece (bedcovers and smaller items alike) and the length needed from top to bottom. If two or more widths are needed, split one piece lengthwise and sew to either side of the other piece to prevent a seam from running down the middle of the top. This method can also be used for the backing of the piece. After pieces are joined, press seams open.

The size and number of quilt blocks will determine how much fabric will be needed. Sketch a small rectangle on a sheet of paper to represent one yard of 45″ wide fabric. Decide how many blocks will fit across and down one yard and how many yards will be necessary for the total number of blocks. Don't forget to add a seam allowance of ¼″ to the sides of all blocks when laying out.

Example: One yard of fabric measures 45″ x 36″ and you have 20 blocks, each measuring 14½″ x 14½″. Divide 14½″ into 36″ which equals 2 blocks with 7″ left over. Now divide 14½″ into 45″ and you will find that three 14½″ blocks will fit across the yardage with 1½″ left over. 3 × 2 = 6 blocks per yard. You need 20 blocks, so divide 6 into 20, equalling 3 with ⅓ yard left over. One-third yard is 12″, not enough for a block, so you will need a total of 3½ yards for your blocks.

Applique and patchwork pieces can be measured in a similar way. First, group together pattern pieces that will be the same color, estimate how large an area each pattern piece covers, and multiply this by the total number of pieces of the one color to be used. Perhaps you have two pieces to be cut from green fabric — a leaf and a stem. The leaf measures approximately two inches by 4 inches with seam allowance added, and there are twenty leaves in all. Multiply 2″ times 20, which will give you a strip 40″ long and 4″ wide. Then do the same for the stem. Add these two together and lay them out on a sketch representing one yard of 45″ fabric. The suggested sketches come in handy when you are shopping for yardage and figuring a cutting layout.

A STITCH IN TIME: REPAIRING OLD QUILTS

Very old quilts are valuable not only as family heirlooms but also as skilled handcraft and art objects, well worth preserving. Perhaps the main consideration when mending old quilts should be to integrate repairs with the original work.

To match fabric, thread, and stitchery on a very old quilt may be difficult. Irregularities in old cloth distinguish it from regulated, machine-made material, for most cloth was homespun and handloomed before 1820. Early handstitching, ironically, was so exact that it takes a skilled needleworker to duplicate it.

Because early dyes were quite fragile, be very careful when cleaning old quilts, taking care to protect them from excessive sunlight. To match fabric or embroidery floss when repairing worn areas, turn the material to the wrong side or bleach them lightly. Better yet, search thrift shops for old fabrics.

When it comes to reinforcing the body of a quilt, invisible strengthening is best, but hand quilting itself adds sturdiness. Consider a new bonded lining for overall strength and nylon net to cover worn patches. Beware of using a sewing machine on delicate, time-worn fabrics. Remove or patch worn areas, adding new fabric with a blind stitch. Rebinding is often the first renewal necessary to protect a worn quilt.

If only part of a quilt is salvageable, you can re-cover and tie it or frame the best portion. Use your imagination to devise decorative ways to display old quilts in a manner that will keep them from wearing out.

Pattern drafting and cutting

The most important aspect of making a pieced or appliqued item is copying, marking, and cutting the pattern pieces properly so that they will be the desired size and fit together correctly. This single activity can mean the difference between a finished project having a smooth, unpuckered appearance or an uneven, poorly fitted look. See step by step illustrations at right.

Drafting patterns. Making a cutting template, or pattern, is simple. Copy your correctly sized design

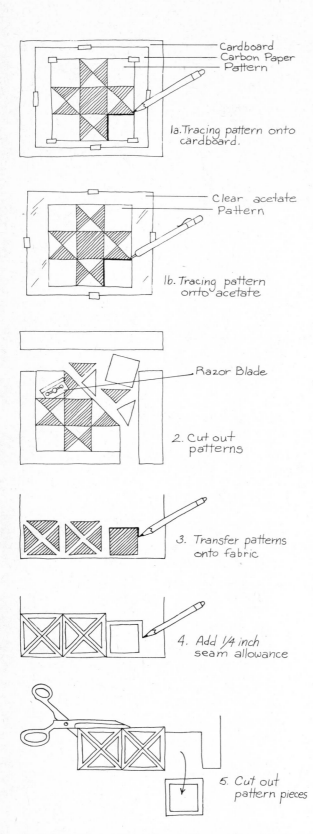

1a. Tracing pattern onto cardboard.

— Cardboard
— Carbon Paper
— Pattern

1b. Tracing pattern onto acetate

— Clear acetate
— Pattern

2. Cut out patterns

— Razor Blade

3. Transfer patterns onto fabric

4. Add 1/4 inch seam allowance

5. Cut out pattern pieces

Step by step procedures *from making cardboard and acetate (plastic) patterns to transferring and cutting them from fabric are shown above. At right, pattern pieces are strung together on a length of thread for safekeeping.*

onto a piece of tracing paper, using a fairly sharp medium-hard pencil. Be as accurate as possible when copying, for any mistake can affect the final look of the design. A triangle, compass, and straight-edge are inexpensive tools that can help to maintain accuracy.

Tape the tissue pattern over a sheet of carbon paper placed on thin cardboard and trace the design onto the cardboard with a sharp pencil. Or lay a thin sheet of clear plastic over the tissue sheet and trace the design with a ballpoint pen. For opaque plastic, transfer as with cardboard. To transfer quilting patterns onto fabric, draw the pattern onto a sheet of butcher paper or newsprint, trace over it with a black felt-tip marker, lay the material to be quilted over the design, tape into place, and trace with a sharp semi-hard pencil. A smooth, hard surface and good lighting can make your job that much easier.

Cutting patterns. With a sharp art knife or razor blade, carefully cut out the plastic or cardboard patterns. The cut patterns will be the exact size of the finished pieces, so remember to add a ¼-inch seam allowance to all sides when laying out and cutting. Mark the name of the pattern on each piece and draw an arrow to indicate how the pattern will fall on the grain of the fabric. A notation as to how many pieces are to be cut in specific colors can also be included.

Lay out the pattern pieces on the wrong side of smooth, ironed fabric, spacing them far enough apart to accommodate a ¼″ seam on each side. Think economically when laying out to save fabric, lay the patterns properly on the grain, and be sure the grain of the cloth is straight. It is better to cut, rather than tear, lengths of cloth because the tension created when cloth rips will pull the grain out of alignment. Draw around each pattern with a sharp, medium-hard pencil, being careful to keep its point right next to *all* edges of the pattern, add seam allowances, and cut out *along seam allowance* with sharp scissors.

To keep patterns from being lost, string matching pieces or whole designs onto a length of thread or put them in envelopes marked with the name of the pattern or the individual piece that they contain (see below).

Some random hints. Because the templates wear down as they are used, becoming inaccurate, cut several cardboard patterns for each piece. Heavy duty thread used in sewing seams or in quilting can be strengthened by dipping the entire wooden spool of thread into a bath of heated paraffin for several minutes. Thread treated in this way will slide more easily when going through several layers of material. When cutting any geometric shape, be sure that at least one side falls on the grain of the fabric for stability.

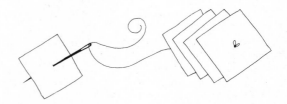

Patchwork

Originally a child of necessity in the world of quiltmaking, patchwork has won a position of permanence and great respect over the years. The endless array of designs and the ingenious use of the scrapbag to create a truly American art form are evidence of the ability inherent in everyone to fashion something beautiful and useful from practically nothing.

At first glance, the word "patchwork" may appear to relate only to the act of *patching* or putting together patches to form a large pieced length of material. But patchwork is actually a term covering several aspects of quilt-making. Technically, *piecework* refers to sewing together bits of fabric, and *patchwork* means 1) the appliqueing of patches of fabric onto a continuous surface to create a pattern or design and 2) the completed pieced block or patch.

Why, then, is patchwork the commonly accepted term for pieced work? Perhaps because it captures the spirit of the ingenuity that went into its own creation. Because this term is commonly accepted as referring to the piecing together of fabric patches, we will continue to apply the word in its current context.

Patchwork designs are as varied as the people who have created them, yet they are all related by their common basis in the principles of geometry and mathematics. An impressive fact is that many people who have created patchwork have known nothing of geometry, yet have produced exceedingly intricate and complex designs by patterns cut from folded paper. A few snips here and there, and presto!—a diamond, square, hexagon, triangle, rectangle, or any one of many designs.

The simplest of patterns are the square, rectangle, and hexagon, cut with the grain of the fabric and therefore stable to work with. Because of their shapes, the diamond, triangle, and parallelogram—not to mention such specialized shapes as trapezoids and stars—must be cut with at least two sides lying on the bias of the material. (See illustration at right.) These patterns are subject to being stretched out of shape when pressed or when worked on, if care isn't taken, and can lead to a pieced top which just won't lie flat. Attempt the simple shapes first; when you have mastered them, tackle bias cut designs.

In a first attempt, the beginner should avoid a design that has curves. Because of the need to match concave curves to convex curves, this work must be done by hand. The curves must be eased together in much the same way as when putting in sleeves when making a garment; in other words, making use of the elasticity of the fabric itself while sewing.

Blocks

Most patchwork patterns are based on an arrangement of elements which, when sewn together, form a square or block. The simplest form of block contains either four or nine squares. Almost all other patterns using the block as a finished shape are based on a similar layout. Look closely at the designs you have seen and ask yourself, "How are they divided visually?" Some of the squares may be divided diagonally once or twice, some may have bars or crosses dividing the elements, and others may have initially confusing designs; but eventually you will be able to distinguish a basic patchwork pattern. A simple sketch may help. Draw out the design in a rough square and divide it into smaller units; it will soon unscramble itself.

This ability to divide and conquer, so to speak, is a very handy tool to have on hand when constructing your block. If you can lay out a grid over the design, you will be able to construct a seemingly complex arrangement of elements very easily, patch by patch. An example may be seen on the opposite page, upper left. This design can be divided into nine patches, each of

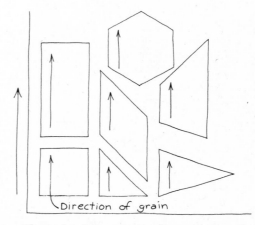

When cutting *out patterns, place pattern pieces on line with the grain of the fabric before marking.*

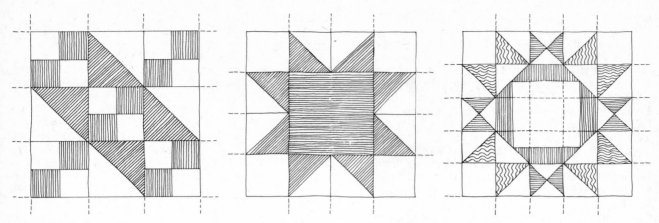

Patchwork blocks *shown above illustrate how block patterns may be divided to simplify construction. Dotted lines indicate* *grid (or divider) marks. At left, Jacob's Ladder; at center, Sawtooth; at right, King David's Crown.*

which may be constructed of either two triangles or four squares. Once each individual patch is made, it is a simple matter to join the patches into rows and the rows into a finished block.

Some blocks contain divisions of 16 and 25 squares, whereas others have four squares divided by a cross, or a design set diagonally into the block. Here again, the 16 and 25 square blocks can be divided by grids into workable patches and then sewn into rows and blocks (upper center, right). If you treat the arms of a cross as patches in themselves, the four-patch designs divided by a cross will become easy (lower left). Diagonal designs may be figured by dividing the square diagonally or by folding the design until the seam pattern emerges (lower center, right).

Making and using patterns

Follow the general directions on pages 12-13 for making patterns, tracing and cutting designs, and laying out pattern pieces. Remember the importance of laying patterns properly on the grain of the material—this will give strength and stability to each piece. Squares and

rectangles should be placed in line with the lengthwise and crosswise threads of the fabric; parallelograms and trapezoids should run with the grain of the fabric; triangles should be laid with the base of the pattern on the grain; diamonds can either be laid with two sides on the grain or with all sides on the bias; and hexagons can fall any which way because of their design. Don't forget to allow for a ¼-inch seam on all sides of each piece. Being as accurate as possible when cutting and joining your pieces will improve the appearance of the finished article. Don't cut a pattern through several layers at once to save time; the pieces will not be accurate.

Assembling patches

Look at your pattern and decide whether you should piece squares into rows or start from the center of the design and work out. Follow a certain order when making the block to avoid mistakes in piecing, laying out all of your pieces and starting from the same point for each similar block. Many blocks can be constructed by machine, especially those with elements that can be stitched into rows. However, sewing by hand will make

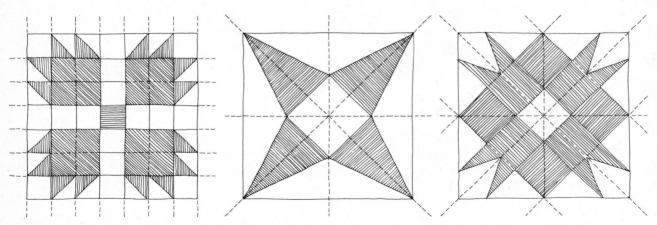

Bear Tracks *(left),* World Without End *(center), and* Royal Star *(right) illustrate ways in which crossed and diagonal designs* *may be simplified. Dotted lines indicate grid patterns used to divide blocks into basic units for ease of construction.*

for more accurate seams and corners and is especially necessary when sewing sharp angles.

The most important thing to do when sewing a seam is to keep your stitches small and even along the seam lines for accuracy in piecing. Work towards eight to ten stitches per inch. Though it will take a little practice, this eventually becomes quite simple.

Unlike other methods of piecing, patchwork does not require matching thread, other than a neutral light for light colors and a neutral dark for dark colors. Keep the length of the thread at about 18 inches (a shorter piece is easier to work with) and use heavy-duty thread. A No. 7 or 8 *sharps* needle is recommended for sewing seams because it is short and facilitates taking short stitches.

Knot the end that is cut off the spool last to prevent tangling, then thread the needle. Pin your pattern pieces together, right sides facing, and check to see that the seam lines marked on each piece are perfectly matched. Take three to four small running stitches along the seam line by rocking the needle up and down through the material with the thumbnail, holding the seam line straight with the opposite thumb and forefinger. Continue to stitch until you've reached the end of the seam, take three backstitches, and knot securely.

Sew several patches together to form a section of the total design, then sew the sections together to form the whole block. Take a backstitch whenever the seam you are sewing crosses another seam, as when sewing together two rows of blocks. This will reinforce those areas. To match corners, points, and angles, place the appropriate pieces right sides facing and pin through the corresponding seams on the seam lines.

Now open the pieces to the right side and check the alignment of the seams. If they aren't quite right, repin and check again until correct. Match the corners and angles first, then the actual seam lines. If several seams come together at one point, you can decrease bulkiness by tapering seams to ⅛ inch before they meet.

Diamonds, triangles, and curves require special handling. Here's how. If you seam triangles into squares or diamonds (depending on their shapes and placement in the design), they can be pieced more easily. In any design using a diamond pattern, there will be a direction in which the diamonds may be sewn to form a strip, or chain. Plot this out according to color arrangement and work the diamonds in these rows, then sew the rows together to form a whole. There are two schools of thought on sewing bias edges: one suggests sewing grain-cut edges to bias edges to stabilize them; the other recommends sewing together diamonds with all edges cut on the bias since these will give in any direction and not cause buckling. Curves may be sewn more easily by folding both concave and convex edges in half, marking then pinning together their centers, and easing half of the curve together until the end is reached. Sew from the end toward the center point, take a backstitch, ease curve together from center to remaining end, and finish sewing.

As each section of the block is finished, press the seams flat in *one* direction—*not* open. Pressing seams flat will leave fewer layers of fabric on the other side of the seam line to quilt through and will make the seams stronger. When the block is finished, turn it on its face and press all of the seams away from the center. Finish all blocks individually before setting anything together so that you may check color arrangement and placement. For ideas on setting blocks together, see section on borders and dividers, pages 17-18.

Making geometric patterns

Squares and rectangles are easy to construct, but you will need some guidelines when making diamonds, hexagons, parallelograms, triangles, and trapezoids. Use a hard leaded pencil for accuracy, and refer to diagrams at bottom of page for construction.

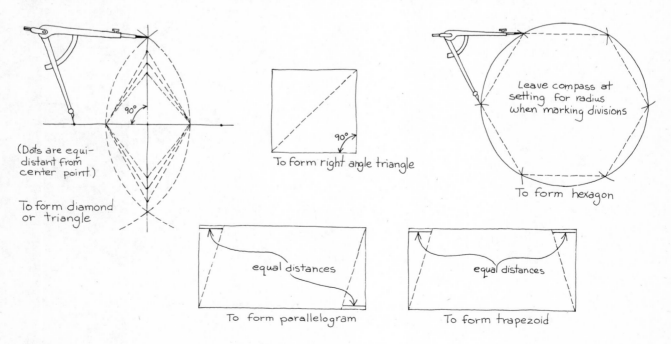

90°

(Dots are equidistant from center point)

To form diamond or triangle

90°

To form right angle triangle

Leave compass at setting for radius when marking divisions

To form hexagon

equal distances

To form parallelogram

equal distances

To form trapezoid

Borders and Dividers

A picture frame, village street plan, checkerboard, or garden path—all are images brought to mind by some of the ways in which a quilt is "set" together and bordered.

The *set* of a quilt refers to the method in which the individual units are joined to make a whole; the *border* means the method in which the entire piece is outlined or "framed," if so desired. The overall design of the quilt will determine what methods should be used to join sections together and whether a border of any kind will be necessary.

Dividers

Blocks may be set in several ways, some of which are shown at the bottom of the page.

Strips. Placed between units, strips create a latticework effect separating complex blocks by plain strips and simple blocks with decorative dividers. An easy way to join blocks into rows is to sew strips vertically between the blocks to make rows and then sew one continuous strip along the top of the row. Do this for all rows, then add another continuous strip to the bottom of the last row, sewing all of the stripped rows together. Strips the length of the entire piece may be alternated with blocks sewn into vertical or horizontal rows for another effect.

Alternating blocks. Plain areas can be alternated with decorated areas and later quilted, or appliqued blocks may be placed between pieced blocks.

Block to block. Several different sizes of rectangles and squares can be successfully joined into one total unit if their sizes are based on multiples of the same number (2 x 3, 2 x 4, or 4 x 4 are all multiples of 2.) Some blocks must be joined edge to edge to create an overall pattern. These are best planned at the start on graph paper for ease of construction.

Diagonal set. This is a rather difficult method of joining, best attempted after completing several pieces joined in a simpler manner. Study the design before determining whether to set block to block or with strips. Often the edges of diagonally set pieces require the insertion of triangles along the outside to "square up" the edges.

o   o   o

Decide tentatively on the method you'll use when you lay out the design on graph paper. You may want to make changes later on but this will give you a starting point.

For ease in working join units first into rows, then lay the rows out on a table top, pin them together to match at corners and seams, and sew up the rows. Sewing by hand makes for accurate joining of corners and rows; machine sewing can make the joined seams stronger. When seaming by machine, tack or baste rows into alignment before sewing. Occasionally, units will be too big or too small for the item to be covered.

 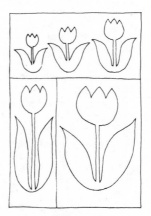 

Quilt blocks *may be set together in four basic ways: strips (left), alternating blocks (center left), block to block (center right), and diagonal set (right), to create a completely joined quilt top suitable to your block design.*

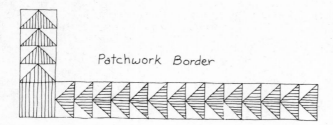

Patchwork Border

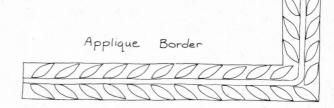

Applique Border

Overcome this problem by taking deeper seams in the big blocks when joining them together or adding strips between too-small blocks.

Borders

Because of their nature, borders are placed in a supporting role, secondary to the central design. The width of this cloth enclosure is generally wider than the width of the blocks in the central design. If no blocks are used, the border takes its width from the major design in the central area.

Borders may be divided into three general types: quilted, patchworked, and appliqued.

Quilted. A very striking border can be created from a simple quilted design repeated around the entire piece. Plan a design on a long strip of paper and lay it out along the edge of the piece to see if it is suitable. When you've chosen your design, punch holes along the pencil lines of the design with the point of a medium-hard pencil, slightly twisting the tip before pulling it out

to punch the next hole. This will mark on the fabric the outline of the design to be followed when you begin to quilt.

Patchwork. These decorations run in single or double strips around the central design. Any patchwork motif that is compatible with the center can be used. An example is shown above, left.

Applique. Again, any design complementary to the central portion of a piece may be used. Running vines are a popular pattern, or you can choose anything from nature in a continual undulating line. See example above, right.

Corners are probably the most difficult portion of a border to plan. Designs should turn the corners smoothly without creating blank areas and without designs from the side strips coming together incorrectly.

You will easily be able to sketch out an appropriate corner design when planning the quilting for a border. However, the corners in patchwork or applique designs must be worked out after the border strips are attached.

The Crazy Patch Quilt

At home in any situation, the crazy patch quilt has been made from a variety of materials to suit a variety of purposes.

Ever wonder where the often-used term "crazy quilt" came from? Well, its origin may be traced to the old worn, patched quilts of our American forebears. Anything hodge-podge, mish-mash, thrown together, or random in a slightly loony way has at one time or another been termed a "crazy quilt." Originally catchall coverlets made purely for necessity from every kind of scrap, crazy quilts eventually reigned as elegant parlor robes in the late 1800s. Graduating from rough homespun scraps to the finery of silks, satins, and brocades, these random patch quilts were delicately hand-decorated with intricate embroidery stitches sewn along the seam lines.

Many kinds of crazy patch quilts can be made, the fabrics ranging from corduroy through wool to silks and velvets. This type of patchwork can be applied to many

different things, as shown by the projects on pages 45, 46, and 48.

Crazy patch may be constructed either by hand or by machine, depending on the surface effect desired. The following methods will show how.

To begin with, crazy patch pieces are sewn to foundation blocks 12″ to 18″ square cut from muslin or old sheeting. While cutting up your scraps into random shapes, think of how you will handle the placement of each color and print on the muslin squares. For examples of methods, see bottom of facing page.

Old-fashioned

Using traditional materials sewn together by hand and embroidered, this method is the most elegant of all.

Keep a pleasing color placement in mind as you pin the scraps to a muslin square, overlapping the edges of the scraps by ½ inch. When everything looks right, turn under each overlapping edge and baste to the muslin foundation. Sew down the turned edges by using cotton floss to make fancy embroidery stitches over the seam lines. This will hold the pieces in place, and the basting stitches may then be removed.

Machine sewn

Although this will look just like the old-fashioned crazy patch, it will take less time to make. Beginning in one corner of a muslin square, place a scrap down and pin it. A second scrap is laid along one inner edge and face down over the first, and a seam is sewn along one edge of the overlap of the first and second scraps. The second scrap is then turned right side up, pinned down, and a third scrap is placed face down over the second scrap. Then a seam is sewn along the edge of the overlap. This is continued until the entire muslin square is covered. A few of the seams will require hand sewing, for it will not be possible to turn them for machine stitching. Turn under the edges and baste down. Now make fancy embroidery stitches with embroidery floss along the seams of the scraps and — surprise! — an "old-fashioned" masterpiece.

Machine zigzag

One scrap is placed on the muslin block and pinned into place. The second piece is placed next to it, slightly overlapping, and top-stitched into place with a narrow zigzag machine stitch. No edges need be turned under.

The second piece is placed next to the first, slightly overlapping and again zigzagged into place. Continue this pattern until the square is filled. Unlike the two methods previously discussed, this one requires patches cut from the same type of material, such as all corduroy or all wool, because of the type of sewing used.

Many crazy patch quilts have been decorated with appliqued figures, pictures sewn onto random patches, or fanciful embroidered designs stitched onto the patches. Various examples of these techniques may be seen on pages 66, 74, and 79.

The procedure for setting together and finishing your crazy patch blocks is the same for each method we've talked about. After all blocks are made up, sew them together into rows and then, being careful to match corners, join rows into one whole piece. Seamlines may be disguised by sewing down small scraps overlapping the seams to break their straight lines. Measure the size of the finished top and cut a piece of yardage slightly larger for backing. Choose a backing material similar to the materials used on the top of the piece. Taffeta, silk, patterned cotton, or flannel are good backing materials.

Crazy patch quilts are tied, rather than quilted, because of the bulkiness of the top. It would be difficult to hand quilt a piece with so many layers of fabric, so the anchoring together of the top, batt, and backing is accomplished by turning the quilt face *down,* laying the batting on, and then the backing. Everything is pinned into place, and yarn or heavy embroidery cotton is used to make ties through all three layers. No ties will show on the front because the needle only catches the muslin backing when a tie is made. For detailed information on tying, binding, and finishing, see pages 28 and 31.

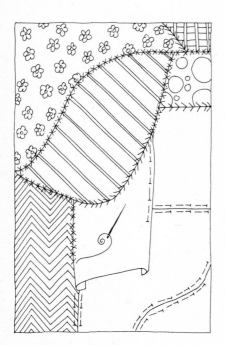 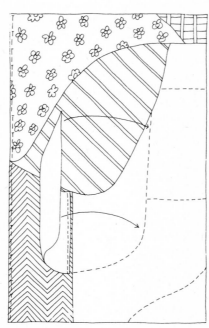 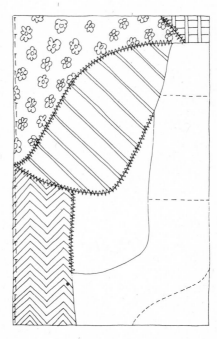

Crazy patch tops *are put together in several ways: old-fashioned (left), machine sewn (center), or machine zigzag (right).*

Hexagonal Patchwork

Kaleidoscopic in its possibilities, this geometric form can become a flower, a star, or an intricate optical illusion.

It's possible to make a variety of fascinating optical designs using only this single shape. Pattern and color are all-important in the arrangement of colored and printed hexagons to create flowers, stars, a honeycomb, and many other geometric designs. So plan your design and color arrangement on graph paper first. Plain fabrics and small prints are best for hexagon use. You can choose from two methods for making hexagonal patchwork—one by machine, one by hand.

Initially a template is made, including a ¼ inch seam all around. Hexagon shapes are cut from yardage or scraps and strung together in the order that they will be used.

Machine sewn

Place two hexagons with their right sides facing and sew along one seam allowance. Sew rows of hexagons in this manner, watching color placement carefully. Join rows together in proper order to complete the top. (See illustrations 1 and 2, below, left.)

By hand

When fabric hexagons are cut, make several dozen hexagons the size of the finished patch from old greet-ing cards or cereal boxes. Lay these cardboard hexagons on the backs of the cloth hexagons and baste the cloth around the cardboard. Make up the hexagons you will use for each geometric motif in this manner and group them together. Then, placing two of them right sides facing, sew one set of edges together, using an overcast stitch. Sew all hexagons around and out from one central hexagon until the motif is complete. (See illustrations 3 and 4 below, right.) When all motifs are completed, connect them together in the desired pattern. It will give strength to the pieces if two backstitches are taken at each crossing seam. Remove the cardboard pieces when all sides of a patch are sewn down.

○ ○ ○

Accuracy is very important when sewing hexagons. Be sure your pattern is even on all sides; hand sewing is the most accurate way of joining the patches.

When the design is finished, remove all basting stitches, turn it on its face and iron all seams out away from the center for easier quilting. The edges of a hexagon patchwork piece will be uneven. You may square off the edges using partial patches or leave the edge as it is. If left uneven, edges may be slipstitched (see page 23) to a backing with edges cut to match.

A hexagon pattern of any size may be constructed by following the directions given on page 16.

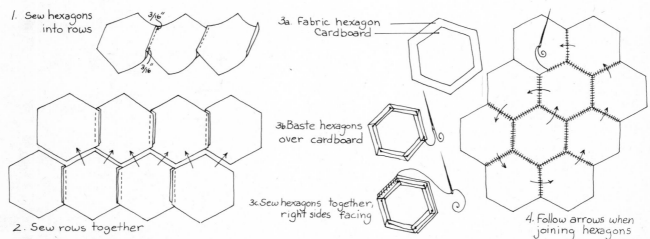

1. Sew hexagons into rows
3/16"
3/16"

2. Sew rows together

3a. Fabric hexagon Cardboard

3b. Baste hexagons over cardboard

3c. Sew hexagons together, right sides facing

4. Follow arrows when joining hexagons

Optical design *using hexagons may be created by machine (steps 1 and 2) and by hand (steps 3 and 4). Be sure to leave* 3/16" *open at each end of each seam to make the joining of rows easier. Openings allow for the crossing of seams.*

The Many Faces of Applique

A surface decoration with many uses, applique can add extra zing to almost anything made from fabric. Many kinds of applique are adaptable to the adornment of a quilted surface. This section will give you all the basic knowledge you'll need to try your hand at any of them.

One of the most versatile techniques in piecework, applique has as many variations and adaptations as you have ideas. It basically amounts to cutting a design from one piece of fabric and *applying* it to the surface of another.

There are many ways in which this can be done: *turned* or *blind applique,* in which the edges of the design are turned under and sewn down invisibly or with decorative stitches; *stuffed applique,* in which batting is stuffed under each appliqued piece to raise it up and make it puffy; *three-dimensional applique,* which is partially attached to the background but has certain areas which are backed and hang free; *iron-on applique,* which is made from commercially available patch kits for clothing repair or from a newly developed bonding material placed between two fabrics and melted into the cloth layers by a hot iron; *Hawaiian applique,* in which one large motif is used as an overall design; and *layered* or *reversed applique,* in which several layers of fabric in different colors are sandwiched together and then cut through to the color desired, turned, and sewn down to create a pattern. All methods shown at right.

Each has myriad design possibilities, of which none is particularly difficult to attempt. By using adaptable designs and materials and practicing certain tried-and-true methods, anyone can easily do applique work.

Materials and equipment

The very basic supplies you'll need include a No. 7 embroidery or millinery needle for stitching, 50 or 60-weight thread in a color to match the applique (or embroidery floss if decorative stitches are to be used), a small scissors with sharp points, a thimble that fits properly for the finger that will be pushing the needle, and suitable fabric.

Almost anything can be used for applique, but non-fraying materials are best. If loosely woven fabrics are used, back them with iron-on bonding to keep them from fraying. Transparent cloth may be backed with lightweight interfacing when sewn down. Certain materials eminently suitable for applique are not so suitable for the washing machine, so determine to what use the piece will be put before deciding on fabrics. Felt is a particularly good fabric for applique work since it

needn't have turned hems and is perfect when small pieces with sharp angles and deep curves (such as hands, flowers, or small details) are needed. However, felt must be drycleaned.

Background fabrics should be compatible with those to be appliqued down, particularly if the piece will often be washed or cleaned.

Frames are often mentioned as absolutely necessary for applique and embroidery, but many fine pieces have been done without one. Wooden hoops come in several sizes and are probably all that are necessary if a frame is desired.

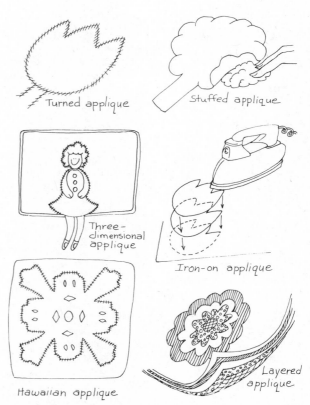

Turned applique

Stuffed applique

Three-dimensional applique

Iron-on applique

Hawaiian applique

Layered applique

Presenting *six commonly used methods of varying the appearance of applique work to create special effects.*

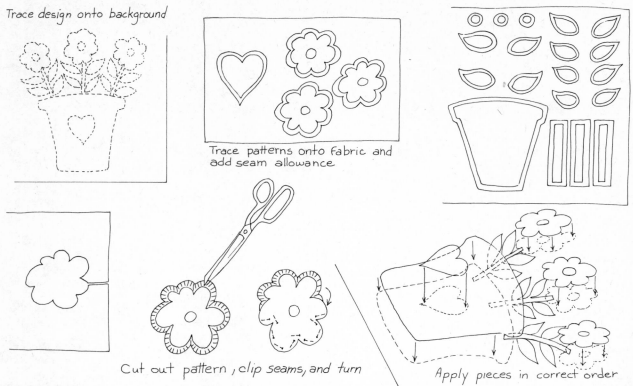

Trace design onto background

Trace patterns onto fabric and add seam allowance

Cut out pattern, clip seams, and turn

Apply pieces in correct order

Four basic steps *of applique: 1. marking design on the background, 2. tracing patterns and adding seams, 3. cutting out* *pattern, clipping seams, and turning edges, and 4. applying applique pieces to background in the proper order.*

Because all fabrics have some give, it's best to have the grain of the applique running with the grain of the background to prevent any stretching or tearing of either fabric. Remember this when laying out and cutting patterns.

Making and preparing patterns

Eventually nearly everything can be used as a design idea once you've learned to handle simple pieces. But keep your first patterns fairly large with simple shapes. When you have chosen your design, made it the correct size, and laid out your idea to your satisfaction on ¼ inch graph paper, follow the general directions for making and cutting patterns given on pages 12 and 13.

Take the pattern pieces for your design and place them on the background material to decide which arrangement and placement works best. Then, with a semi-hard lead pencil (on dark fabrics use a white-leaded pencil), trace the outline of each pattern piece onto the background as a guide to follow when sewing down the applique. Now trace the applique patterns onto the front of your chosen fabric, remembering to leave enough space between each individual piece for a ¼ inch seam. (See upper left, center, and right.)

Cut out the pattern pieces, including the seam allowance. Clip any curved or angled areas almost to the pencil line and turn under the seam allowance to the pencil line in any of the following ways: 1) lay the

template over the applique piece on the wrong side of the fabric and iron back all seams around the edges of the template; 2) finger-press the seam allowance under and baste with white thread, leaving free the edges which will be overlapped by other edges in the design; 3) pin the applique piece to the background and turn under edges as you work. (See lower left.)

The seam allowance on curves should be clipped, eased under gradually, then basted. Using materials with accommodating characteristics will make this much easier. Circles may be turned by running a thread around the outside edges, gathering slightly, and pressing the circle flat.

To lay on the applique pieces, first decide in which order they will be sewn down. Try to position bottom pieces first and then fit in the middle and top pieces. Pin everything into place, give the arrangement one last check, and then baste it all down with white thread. (See lower right.)

Attaching the applique

An applique piece may be sewn down in a variety of ways: running stitch, slipstitch, buttonhole stitch, or invisible stitch. Examples are shown on the facing page.

Since each stitch gives the piece a certain look, decide which feeling you want. Using a No. 7 or 8 embroidery or millinery needle, begin to stitch along the outline of the piece, using thread in a matching color. For contrasting effect, embroidery floss is better than regular thread. When ending or starting a thread, always make knots on the wrong side of the background fabric. When you have completed your stitching, remove basting thread and, placing the piece face down on a padded surface, press gently.

○ ○ ○

Here are a few tips on handling special problems:

Corners and points. Stitch to within ¼ inch of the corner or point, backstitch one stitch, and turn the corner under. Then push the protruding raw edge back under with the tip of your needle and stitch around the corner or point, tucking with the needle tip, if necessary. For acute angles, divide the design into several pattern pieces to eliminate the sharp corners. An example are the fins and tail of a fish. Cut one pattern for the body and separate patterns for each fin and the tail.

Floral vines and stems. Commercially made bias tape can be used for vines and flower stems, or strips can be cut 1¼ inch wide on the bias of a piece of cloth and folded twice for an overall width of ½ inch. When sewing these strips into curves, sew down the inner part of a curve first and then coax the outer curve into place. Keep the width of a stem constant.

Embroidered details. Some parts of an applique design may be too small for anything but embroidered decoration. Do any decorative stitching last, after everything has been sewn down.

○ ○ ○

Information on setting together your work and bordering it may be found on pages 17 and 18.

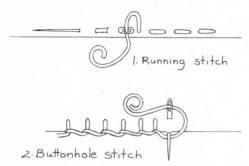

1. Running stitch

2. Buttonhole stitch

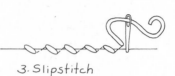

3. Slipstitch

4. Invisible stitch

Basic stitches *for attaching applique work to its background include: 1. running stitch, 2. buttonhole stitch, 3. slip stitch,* *and 4. invisible stitch. Running and buttonhole stitches are decorative; invisible and slipstitch are purely functional.*

Applique by Sewing Machine

The whirr-r of your sewing machine can make applique go very quickly. Use these convenient methods to speed your work along.

If you're the kind of person who likes to get immediate results in what you're doing or an end product that can really take the wear and tear of constant use, then you'll probably be very interested in the use of the sewing machine for applique work. There's no need for a machine with many fancy attachments or special parts; even machines with only a straight stitch can be used creatively in applique work.

The machine itself may be used in two ways—either with the presser foot on or with the foot removed and the feed-dogs dropped. With the foot on at very low pressure and the stitch length set at 20-25 stitches per inch, either a very close straight stitch or a satin-like zigzag stitch may be achieved. When the foot is removed, the feed-dogs dropped, and the presser foot lever lowered, you will have complete freedom of move-

ment with either the straight or the zigzag stitch.

The instruction manual for your machine will undoubtedly contain information on machine applique that should be read before you use your machine for applique work. Some of the more expensive models have attachments for creating decorative stitches. These can be used to add variety to your appliqued shapes. Remember that machine stitches will flatten the surface of a fabric, whereas hand stitching will make it puff up.

Sewing down applique pieces by machine may be done in the following four ways: (A sheet of typing paper should be placed underneath the two thicknesses of material to prevent gathering and bunching. Pin it into place when you pin down the applique piece, sew through it when stitching, and tear away when finished.)

1) Trace your design onto the fabric and add about

⅛" to ¼" around the piece when cutting it out. Pin the piece securely in place on the background and, using a zigzag stitch wide enough to cover the extra fabric allowance, sew the piece down along the edges. 2) Trace your design onto the fabric and add 2" all around. Pin the piece in place and zigzag along the pencil outline of the design. When finished, carefully clip away the excess cloth with a pair of sharp-pointed scissors.

3) Trace your design onto fabric and add ¼" seam allowance. Cut out the piece, clip the edges, then turn them under and press. Pin securely and top-stitch into place with a straight stitch. 4) Trace design onto fabric and onto a sheet of iron-on interfacing. Cut out both and iron the applique and interfacing sandwich onto the background fabric. Zigzag over the raw edges to finish. (All methods are shown below.)

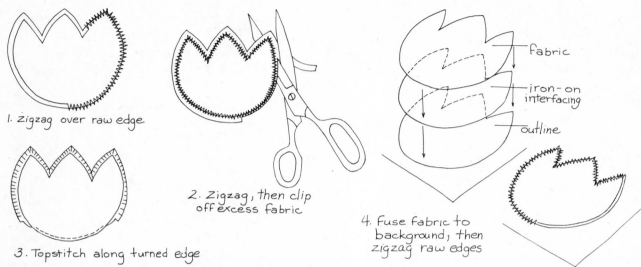

1. Zigzag over raw edge

2. Zigzag, then clip off excess fabric

3. Topstitch along turned edge

4. Fuse fabric to background, then zigzag raw edges

A good tool *for applique work: your sewing machine. Zigzag and regular stitches can be used to sew down applique pieces in four ways, all shown above. Iron-on applique makes work go faster and holds applique firmly in place.*

SHARING AND SHOWING QUILTS

Quilting instructors have only two requirements to meet for "certification": one is a love for the art; the other, a growing knowledge about it. To share quilting with others, you should organize all available resources—books, patterns, articles, samples, and other people who are knowledgeable about quilting.

In order to let the world know there are quilting classes available, plan an advertising campaign. A continuing ad asking for scraps to be donated to quilting classes brings in many boxes of material and at the same time publicizes the classes. Send each prospective student an information sheet and a map. About eight students per class is a good number.

Ask your students to bring a pair of scissors and to dress comfortably. You can hold classes in your home, convert a garage, or use local community centers. You'll need storage space for boxes of material, batting, and extra frames; a sewing machine; ironing space; and a large work table.

Use the first lesson to introduce students to what they're going to cover. Don't discourage them by displaying too many elaborate, long-term projects.

Your students will feel a sense of accomplishment if they practice on sampler squares that can be made into pot holders, pillows, or pin cushions. If the class is working on a complete quilt, it's fun to have a drawing at the end of classes to see who wins it. Eight lessons are usually enough to cover basic quilting techniques. The fewer "rules" there are to follow, the more

scope there'll be for creativity. Advanced classes could include making Cathedral Window or border print quilts, Hawaiian cushions, tablecloth quilts, painted quilt tops, and repairing old quilts.

It's fun to hold small quilt shows after the classes are completed to which students can bring their families and friends. If you enjoy giving quilt shows, they can also be produced on a larger scale as money-making projects. Charge an admission fee or sell some of the quilts — baby quilts are very popular.

Write to various people who quilt, charitable organizations, and quilting supply stores to arrange for quilting materials to be on sale. You'll need to reserve a room for your show several months in advance. Organize helpers to plan the show, employ a night watchman, and contact the custodian to check on details. Notify newspapers and other publicity agencies well ahead of time.

It's fun to have as many entries as possible, but be sure to work out an identification system with claim checks. Type information about the quilt, its maker, and date made on a card and attach it to the quilt.

Remember that visitors usually enjoy demonstrations; you can give a comforter quilted during the show as a door prize. An added attraction might be a section on Hawaiian quilts. One useful idea is a clearing-house bulletin board for quilters who are offering their services and people who are looking for quilting experts or a place where old quilts may be repaired.

Quilting

A modern definition of quilting might well be "getting it all together."
You will literally be joining all of the separate units (backing, batt, and top)
into one cohesive piece. Quilting may be whatever you wish; lavish in
design or plain for the sake of practicality.

Gradually a subtle dimension unlimited in its possibilities appears in your work as beautiful patterns and effective designs evolve. Certain areas may be fat and puffy while others, being closely quilted, have ridges and deep furrows. Lines, curves, scrolls, circles, or anything pictorial can be quilted into a beautiful surface design, giving character and texture to what was once a flat, formless surface. Imagine the variations open to you!

Equipment

A list of necessities for quilting includes heavy-duty or quilting thread, No. 7 or No. 8 *between* (or quilting) needles, T-pins, upholstery pins or safety pins, a small pair of scissors, a comfortable thimble, beeswax to strengthen your thread, semi-soft lead pencil for marking your design, gum eraser to correct mistakes, and a whisk brush to remove eraser rubbings. Don't forget your handy rubber balloon for pulling needles that stick.

Depending on your individual inclination, decide at this point whether you will use a quilting frame, a hoop, or quilt without a frame. If you decide to use a frame, an inexpensive yet efficient one can easily be constructed. You will need the following items: two lengths of 1" x 2" knot-free fir or pine as long as the width of your quilt and two lengths as long as the length of your quilt; four 3" C-clamps; strips of ticking or denim, enough to cover all four length of wood; a box of ½" carpet tacks and hammer or a staple gun; four straight-backed chairs. Materials can be found at a lumberyard or hardware store. Cover all four lengths of wood with the ticking, overlapping the material, then stapling or tacking it down every two inches. See lower left.

Cover the top rungs of the chairs with towels to protect them and place the shorter boards across the backs of each pair of chairs. Then lay the longer boards across the tops of the shorter boards. Place C-clamps at each corner, clamp the overlaps together, and tie the corners to the chairs with old nylon stockings. Your frame is now complete; the next step is to set in your quilt.

A fully constructed frame is shown at lower right.

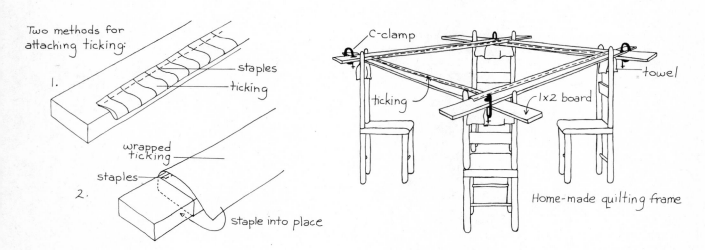

Ticking *may be attached to 1 x 2's by two methods (above left). At right, a homemade quilting frame is shown set up for* work. Four ladderback chairs provide support, and towels protect chair backs from being scratched.

When not in use, the frame may be dismantled and stored in a closet: if a quilt is on the frame, it may be leaned against a wall or rolled up like a scroll and placed in a corner.

If you decide to use a quilting hoop or to quilt without a frame, several things make a big difference in the look of the finished piece. Anything done off the frame must be basted to within an inch of its life if you don't want a sagging, drooping, bunched-up quilt. Everything should be thoroughly thread-basted or pinned every four inches with large safety pins. Check the back of the piece frequently to see if the backing needs to be smoothed. It's not easy to have an overall view of the piece as it is being worked on in a hoop or your lap, so lay the piece out frequently to judge your progress, checking for gathers or bunching on the backing.

Marking the quilting design

Unlike the top of a set-in quilt, a quilt top done off the frame is marked for the quilting design before all three layers are put together. The marking procedure is the same for both types, whether done on a table, the floor, or in a frame.

Quilting patterns are chosen with an eye to the original design of the quilt top. A patchwork design usually requires quilting along the outlines of each individual piece or around the major motifs. Certain patchwork pieces having strips or squares where no patchwork exists may be filled with a compact design having all of its parts within the square and with a running pattern moving along the strips or around the border. Appliqued tops have specific design areas, usually outline-quilted, and large areas of open space that may be filled with a design appropriate to their size and the mood of the overall quilt design. Quilting patterns for plain tops usually begin from the center and radiate outward with a special design used on the border. Remember that certain types of batt will require close quilting and plan accordingly. For a list of fillers, see page 10.

These are only suggestions. Anything may be used as a pattern and may be placed on the quilt top in any order. Use whatever best complements your design. Household ware, office equipment, design books, or magazines, all can be used to create designs and make patterns. A great variety of traditional patterns is also available. Check with your local library, looking under needlecrafts or crafts.

Lay your top out on a smooth, clean, hard surface for marking. Make cardboard or tissue paper patterns of your designs. Cardboard templates are placed on the top and outlined with a medium-soft pencil. Tissue paper may be laid over the top and punctured along the pencil line with a soft lead pencil, leaving dots to indicate the quilting lines. Mistakes can be removed with an art gum eraser. For straight line quilt patterns, use a yardstick for marking or lay down lengths of masking tape to follow as you stitch. Pull the tape off when you have finished quilting along it.

It will probably be difficult to reach the center portion of a set-in quilt for marking. Don't worry. After the quilt has been rolled up a couple of times, you'll be able to finish the pattern easily.

Preparation for quilting

Two basic approaches may be used. *Hoop and off-frame:* lay out the backing, wrong side up, on a flat surface, and place the batt on top of it. Smooth it out. Next, place the top right side up over the batt and adjust it. Some of the backing and batt should show around the edges of the quilt top.

Now baste or pin. Using a contrasting thread, take large stitches through all three layers in the pattern shown below or pin through all three layers using glass-headed pins (sink the points into the batt when pinning) or large safety pins. After you've made one last check for wrinkles, you're ready to place the piece in a quilting hoop or to work it in your lap. This method is also used to prepare a quilt for commercial quilt frames. *To set into a frame:* Measure and mark the center points of each length of 1 x 2. Now, mark the center points of each side of your backing material. Matching their centers, pin each mark on the backing to the corresponding mark on the proper 1 x 2 and pin it securely to the ticking with T-pins or upholsterers' pins. Working out from these center points, pin the backing in place at intervals of three inches out to the corners. Set the pins parallel to the edge of the 1 x 2 and sink the points of the pins into the ticking to avoid being pricked.

When pinning is completed, square up the frames, stretch the backing taut, and reclamp. Now place the batting over the backing and adjust it to fit. If batting comes in strips, loosely baste the strips together.

Find the centers of all four edges of the quilt top and mark them. Lay the top over the batting, match its cen-

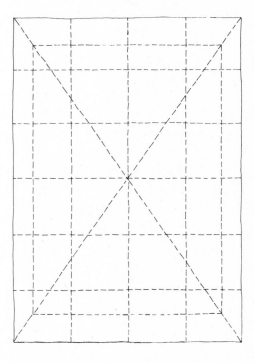

Dotted lines *indicate basting pattern used to stabilize the three layers of a quilt: top, batt, and backing.*

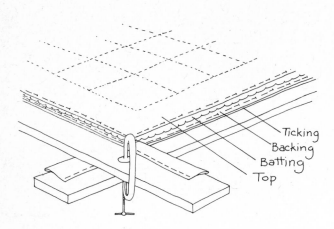

Setting a quilt *into the frames. Dotted lines indicate a quilting pattern marked on the quilt top with a lead pencil.*

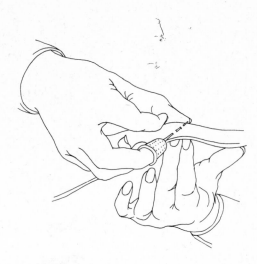

Quilting stitches *are taken through all three layers, working toward yourself and using your thumb as a guide.*

ter marks to those marked on the 1 x 2's, and pin as you pinned the backing. See illustration at top left.

Quilting

Find a point about 12 inches in from the edge of the quilt where you can begin to make your stitches. Using a No. 7 or No. 8 quilting needle threaded with an 18-inch-long single strand of quilting or heavy-duty thread knotted at one end, push the tip of the needle through only the top layer about 1 inch from your starting point. Bring the point of the needle back up at the starting point and pull it all the way through until the knot is resting on the surface. Tug on the needle until the knot pops through the top and is hidden.

Begin to take short running stitches along the quilting lines through *all three layers,* working toward yourself. Take very small stitches, starting with the needle in an up and down position, and pushing the needle at an angle with the thimble-covered middle finger toward the thumb, holding the material flat before the needle. The opposite hand is held beneath the quilt against the backing to guide the needle tip when it pierces the back. The forefinger and middle finger push up against the backing to help the needle tip take a short stitch before returning to the face of the quilt. See illustration at top right of page.

Take three to four stitches at a time, making sure that the needle has gone through to the back of the quilt and that you are pulling the thread tight. Though it will take practice to make your stitches even and small, concentrate on *even* stitching and try for eight to ten stitches per inch. You'll make it sooner than you think. Thick or stiff material will force you to take larger stitches, but it is easier to quilt them if the needle is worked in an up and down position.

To fasten off an end, double back through the top layer about five or six stitches, as though you were quilting backward through all three layers. Then go down into the batt and take a very long stitch before returning the needle and thread to the surface. Take a

tiny stitch, sink the needle again into the batt, come back to the surface, and clip the thread close to the fabric. The end will sink back into the quilt.

Rolling a set-in quilt

The greatest width that may be comfortably worked on a set-in quilt is about a 1-foot-wide strip around the four sides. When this has been quilted, it will be time to roll the quilt. It takes two people to roll a quilt, so find a willing helper who is fairly strong. Loosen the C-clamps on 2 adjacent corners and unpin the back and top from the frame as far as you have quilted. Now face the quilt, brace the side frames against your body, and roll the finished portion under until you reach the unquilted part. Square up the frames, pull everything taut, and reclamp the corners. See illustration below.

When your quilt is finished, remove all basting stitches or pins. If the quilt is on the frame, unpin the backing and top from the frames, unroll the rest of the quilt, and remove the entire piece from the frames. See pages 31 to 33 for suggestions on how to bind your piece.

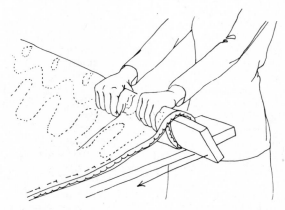

Brace quilt frame *tightly against your body to hold it steady and roll quilted portion under and away from you.*

The Tie that Binds

Looking for a quick way to make up a quilt or comforter? Try tying.

This method of joining the three layers of a quilt makes use of short lengths of tied yarn or floss instead of quilting to hold everything together.

Use an old blanket, dacron batt, or a sheet blanket for filler because ties are usually widely spaced and won't hold cotton batting in place.

Determine the size you will make your tied comforter and prepare the top and backing according to suggestions on pages 14 to 24. When they are ready to use, either put the pieces into a quilting frame (see page 26) or lay the backing on the floor face down, place the filler over the backing, lay on the top, right side up, and pin-baste all three layers together thoroughly.

A quilt may be tied in several ways. You can mark with a ruler every four inches across and down the top and tie at the marks; you can use the design on the comforter top to determine where your ties should be placed; or you can create your own random tying pattern. Whatever method you follow, don't leave any large spaces untied.

Using a long sharp yarn needle, thread it with about 2 yards of yarn or floss and double the strand. Don't tie a knot in it. At the points you've marked on the top, go straight down through all three layers, leaving about 2 inches of yarn on the top, and come right back up to the surface about ¼ inch away. (See illustration.) Cut through the yarn, tie it in a square knot, clip to about 1 inch, and go on to the next tie. Before you know it, everything will be tied and your quilt will almost be completed. For ideas on finishing the edges, see pages 31 to 33.

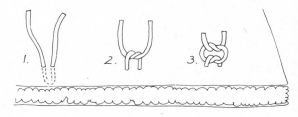

Square knot *holds yarn ties securely.*

Variations on a Theme

There is more to quilting than you may suspect. English Padding, Stuffed Applique, and Trapunto are three methods that take off from traditional quilting to create unique effects all their own.

An unusual look can be achieved when particular areas of a piece are raised or padded in contrast to the rest of the surface. This may be done by stuffing only certain areas of a quilt-stitched surface, by running strands of yarn through parallel lines of stitching to create linear designs or by placing filler beneath applique pieces before they are completely sewn down.

Materials best suited for these types of quilting include any fabric that is soft and pliable with a pleasing surface texture. Plain fabrics are preferred, for the real character of these methods lies in the raised motif rather than in the printed design on a fabric. Backing materials include netting, loosely woven muslin, voile, cheesecloth, or dress lining; all make it easy to either part the threads for stuffing or to run a large needle and strands of yarn through the backing.

The basic method amounts to drawing a design to be stuffed or outline-corded on the backing, basting the backing to the wrong side of the surface material, stitching through both layers along the lines of the design, then either stuffing or cording the design into shape. In general, these techniques may all be speeded along through the use of the sewing machine. The only difference in appearance will be the overall look of the surface stitching.

English padding

Choose a design with large areas to fill and trace it onto the lining with a semi-soft lead pencil. Baste the lining to the surface material, wrong sides facing, and sew by hand or by machine along the pencil lines in small, even backstitches or running stitches. When all stitching is completed, part the threads of the lining within the design with a knitting needle until there is a good-sized opening and stuff bits of loose dacron batting under the lining to pad the design area.

Work the stuffing into corners and small areas of the design with a bodkin or thin wooden dowel, then smooth the threads of the lining back into place. Try not to stuff too heavily or the surface will become stiff. If the lining won't pull apart, use a seam ripper to make a slit, being careful not to tear the surface fabric. When you've stuffed the piece, sew the slit closed with a whipstitch (see illustration 1, below). English padding can be applied to many items. An example may be seen on page 44.

Stuffed applique

This method is not dependent on quilting for its effect but rather on the addition of a filler to each individual applique piece before it is completely stitched down. Applique pieces are prepared as usual (see pages 21 to 23) and are sewn into place until two-thirds of the piece is secured. Then bits of dacron batt are stuffed under the piece to raise it slightly and the stitching is completed to attach the piece to the surface (see illustration 2, below). An example can be found on page 42.

Trapunto, or Italian quilting

Originally a surface decoration used in southern areas where warmth is not a prerequisite for quilting, trapunto may be used to create intricate scroll and interlocking linear designs. Initially, a design is transferred to lining material, which is then basted to the surface material, wrong sides facing. The outline of the design is sewn through both layers, then another line is sewn parallel to the first line, ¼ inch away.

When all of the design and all parallel lines are sewn, thread a large, blunt yarn darning needle with three or more strands of acrylic yarn (it slides easily) and start at a corner or on the edge of the design. Run the needle through the lining into the ¼-inch-wide channel until the top of the needle comes back up through the lining. Pull the needle and yarn through until only a short end remains where the needle first entered. Put the needle back into the channel through the same hole where the needle came out, if possible (see illustration 3, below), and continue to fill the ¼ inch channels in this manner. If you reach a sharp angle of the design, come up through the lining, leave a little loop of yarn at that point in case of shrinkage, and sink the needle back in. The loop will give the angle a good shape.

To finish these types of quilting, place a backing cut to size over the piece, right sides facing, pin into place, seam around three sides and part of the fourth, turn, stuff if desired, and slipstitch the opening closed.

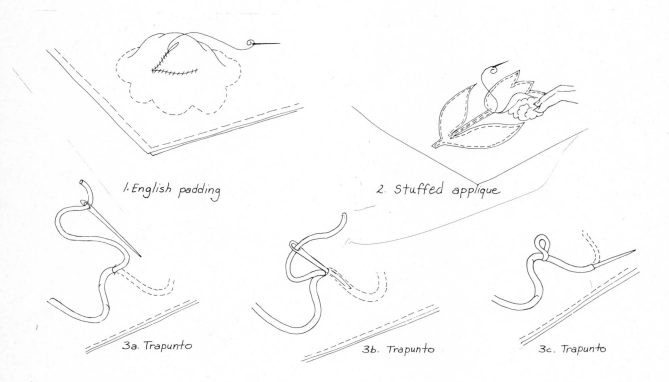

1. English padding

2. Stuffed applique

3a. Trapunto

3b. Trapunto

3c. Trapunto

Extra puffiness is added to your piece by using either English padding, stuffed applique, or trapunto. Both batting and strands of yarn produce a raised effect on the surface of a quilt top or smaller item, creating a unique appearance.

Sew-As-You-Go Quilting

*If your free time is sandwiched between other activities, you can still
patch and quilt. Here's a quick, easy way to make your work portable and convenient.*

There are probably quite a few people who would enjoy quilting but who have neither the time for it nor the space for a quilting frame or hoop. Well, surprise— there is a way for you to make beautiful quilted items piece by piece without a lot of room. It's called "sew-as-you-go quilting." Portable, easy, convenient, and quick, this method may be taken up at your leisure whether you are sitting in your living room, riding in a car, or waiting for an appointment.

The basic idea of sew-as-you-go is to complete individual units (blocks, triangles, squares, or hexagons), which are then joined into a total piece.

Individual blocks

Very similar to the block by block method discussed in our patchwork section, this technique uses a square as its basic unit. A single patchwork or applique block, a square of batting, and a square of backing material are all cut the same size. The three are placed together as illustrated below, step 1, sewn on three sides, turned, and the fourth side is slipstitched shut. The blocks are then individually quilted. When all squares have been finished, they may be joined by slipstitching or by using the zigzag machine stitch to join the butted edges. These quilts usually require no binding and may be decorated by covering the seam lines with braid, bias, rickrack, strips of material, or embroidery. (See illustration 2, below.)

Puff blocks

This method fills individual triangles and squares, which are then joined together to form a block or an overall design. Two of each shape are cut (one for backing and one for the front), placed right sides facing, partially seamed together, turned, stuffed with loose dacron batting, and sewn shut. When all units are finished, they are slipstitched or zigzagged together. The same technique may be applied to hexagons. (See illustration 3, below.) This method produces a beautiful effect, all thick and fluffy, with each patch standing individually.

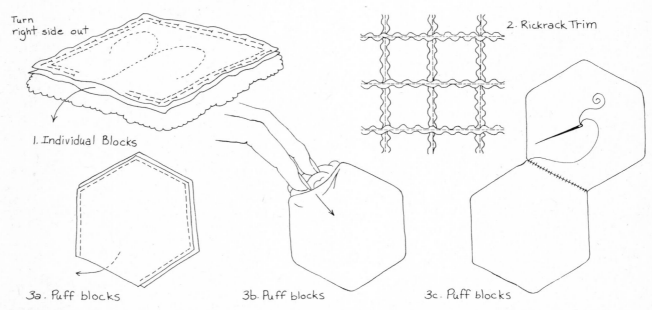

Turn right side out

1. Individual Blocks

2. Rickrack Trim

3a. Puff blocks

3b. Puff blocks

3c. Puff blocks

Sew-as-you-go *makes quilting go quickly. Both individual blocks and puff blocks of triangles, squares, or hexagons are* *stuffed, turned, and quilted individually, then joined by hand-sewing or by machine zigzag into one piece.*

The Finishing Touches

To add beauty and durability to your finished piece, try any one of the suggestions for finishing and binding found in this section.
A central theme may be set off perfectly by the choice of just the right edging, binding, trim, or flounce.

Since different items require different methods of trimming and binding, the edges of a quilted or patch-worked piece may be finished in a variety of ways. To decide which method best suits your piece, lay it out on the floor, step away from it, and with a critical eye balance one type of binding against another as to its effectiveness in finishing off your design. Visualize what each will look like with your work and then make a decision. Remember when working with a binding that it will probably wear out more quickly than any other part of the piece, so it's a good idea to use a double thickness of binding, no matter what method you decide to use.

Binding with the backing

If you have an excess of backing left around the edges, you may use it to bind your quilt. Cut the extra backing so that it is an even width all around, fold in a ½-inch wide hem, and crease it into place. Bring this backing around to the front of the piece and pin it firmly into place in a straight line. This may be sewn down by machine or by hand, removing the pins as you go.

Binding with the top

Extra material in a top may be used to cover and finish raw edges in the same manner that you use extra backing to bind edges. Follow directions for binding with the backing, but turn the excess to the back of the piece to finish.

Excess batting left over when your piece has been quilted may be rolled up along the edges and covered with any extra backing or top material for a puffy edge.

Making a reversible piece

The top and backing of a piece may be sewn together with an invisible stitch, giving a finished look to both sides. To achieve this, trim both the top and backing until they are even; turn the top hem around the batt and under, then turn under a hem on the backing until both folds meet. Pin them together and sew along the folds using an invisible stitch (see illustration at right).

Using trims for a binding

Use the technique for making an invisible edge to add a distinctive trim of ruffles, braid, triangles, or cording.

Ruffles are wide strips of cloth folded in half lengthwise and gathered along the raw edge to fit the sides of the piece. Lay the ruffle along the edge of the top only, right sides facing, raw edges together. Sew ¼-inch in from the raw edge by machine. Turn the ruffle right side up, turn the edge of the backing around the batting edge, lay the sewn line of the top and ruffle down onto the turned edge of the backing, pin into place, and sew by hand.

The edge of a length of braid may be secured in much the same way. Triangles are made from 3-inch squares of material folded twice diagonally, pinned between the edges of the top and the backing, and topstitched by machine. Cording may be attached by covering it with a strip of material, which is then inserted between the edges of the top and backing and sewn into place. Buy a thick length of cording long enough to cover all edges of the piece. Measure and cut strips of material wide enough to cover the cord plus 2 inches. Turn under a hem along the edges of the top and backing, encase the cord in the strip of material, insert the raw edges of the covered cording between the top and backing, pin into place, and topstitch along the turned edge of the top with a zipper-foot to hold everything in place.

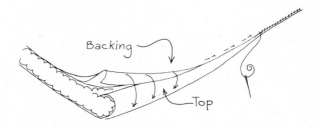

A reversible quilt can show *both sides beautifully if its edges are finished with an invisible stitch.*

Bias binding

This edging is made from either commercially available 1-inch-wide bias tape, or homemade bias tape. Commercially made bias tape is opened up, placed with one raw edge along the raw edge of the top, stitched along the fold line, folded over the edge to the back, and slipstitched on the folded-under edge (see illustration 1, below). Homemade bias is cut from approximately 1 yard of material similar to that used in the piece itself (see illustration 2, below). If you decide to make bias strips for your work, cut them about 2½ inches wide, sew the strips end to end, and fold them in half lengthwise (see illustration 3, below). Trim the raw edges of your piece so that they are even and straight, but leave enough dacron batt to make the edge puffy. Now, lay the raw edges of the folded bias tape along the edge of the top of the piece, pin into place, and sew ¼ inch in from the raw edge. One-quarter inch before reaching the corners, stop sewing and leave 2 inches of overhang before cutting off the strip. Go on to next side, following same steps for the first edge.

Complete the remaining edges in the same manner. Next, turn the piece on its face, grasp the fold of the bias tape, pull it over the raw edges of the tape and the piece to the backing, and pin it securely in as straight a line as you can manage (see illustration 4, below). Sew the tape by hand, using a blind hemstitch. When you reach the corners, you may miter them by folding them under at a 45° angle to the corner on the front

and the back, and, clipping off excess material, sewing them with an invisible stitch (illustration 5, below).

Another method of finishing corners may also be used. (See illustrations 6a, b, and c, below.) When all tape is sewn into place on the top, turn one folded edge of the bias tape on the long sides of the quilt to the back and pin into place. Trim off the corner overlap of this piece (6a). On the remaining bias strips, fold the raw edge around the corner and hold it there while you pull the rest of the bias strip to the back and pin it into place (6b, c). This will hide the raw edge and give reinforcement to the corners of your piece.

Ruffled or box-pleated flounce

Some bedcovers seem to take on an added sparkle when complemented by ruffles or pleats. The same is true for quilts and patchwork spreads. The base for these flounces can be an old sheet or a length of extra-wide muslin sheeting material big enough to cover the top of your boxspring plus 1½ inches on each side for seam allowance. Measure the boxspring length and width and make up a flat sheet to fit.

Now, measure along the foot of the bed and one side. Then add the measurements together, doubling the side measurement to include the length of the opposite side of the bed. Multiply the final figure by three to give the *length* necessary for pleats or ruffles. Measure from the top of the boxspring to the floor and add 3 inches for width of ruffle or pleat plus seam and hem.

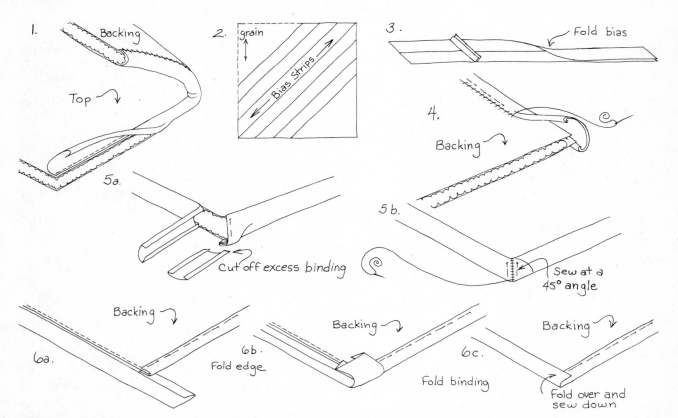

Binding or finishing *edges: (upper left) commercial bias binding, (center right) homemade bias binding, (lower center) mitered corners, and (bottom) turned corners. Bias strips are cut on the diagonal to give extra stretch.*

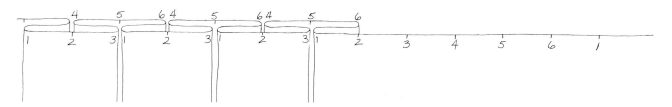

Mark edges of box pleat fabric every two inches, numbering from one through six. Repeat until end is reached. Make pleat folds on numbers 1, 3, 4, and 6 until all pleats are folded. Use a 2″ square of cardboard for a pattern.

Decide how much 45-inch-wide fabric will be necessary to make the ruffles or pleats by dividing 45 into the total measurement of the three sides of the bed to determine how many 45-inch-wide strips sewn together will make a long enough piece. Add an extra 1½ feet for seams. Take the resulting number and multiply it times the boxspring to floor measurement to find how many total inches of fabric will be necessary.

Cut the fabric across the width and join the pieces into one long continuous strip. Make a 1½-inch hem all along one side of the strip and on both ends.

To make ruffles. Lay a length of string along the raw edge of the strip and zigzag over the string, being careful not to sew through it. When finished, gather the strip by pulling up the string until it fits the three sides of the bed and the ruffles are evenly spaced. With right sides facing, pin the raw ruffled edge to the edges of the muslin sheet on three sides. Place on the bed to check for correct length from boxspring to floor. Sew the ruffles to the sheet with a 1½-inch seam. Turn and place over the boxspring.

To make box pleats. Cut a square of cardboard 2 inches by 2 inches for a template. Lay this at one corner on the raw edge of the strip and mark off two inch divisions. Do this for the entire length of the strip. Starting at one end, number the pencil marks from one to six until you reach the other end. Make your folds as shown in illustration above, on numbers one, three, four and six to create box pleats. Pin the pleats into place and continue along the edge until the entire length is pinned and pleated. With the right sides facing, pin the raw pleated edge to the edges of the muslin sheet, adjusting the placement of the pleats so that the spaces between two pleats fall at the corners of the foot of the bed. Place the sheet over the boxspring to check the correct length of the pleats from floor to boxspring. Sew raw pleated edge to the sheet with a 1½-inch seam. Turn and place over boxspring.

STORIES AND SUPERSTITIONS

To learn about quilting is to become aware of the past through other quilters' eyes. Even the names of patchwork patterns tell volumes about a bygone way of life.

Who would believe a quilt could be a historical document? Consider such names as Whig Rose, Clay's Choice, White House Steps, Lincoln's Platform, and Old Tippecanoe. These patterns recall important political figures and events. The Mexican Cross pattern, from the 1840s, is a haunting reminder of an almost forgotten war.

The daily life of early America was nearly as dramatic as the political arena. Pioneer days echo in patterns like Indian Trail, Bear's Paw, Log Cabin, Prairie Queen, Rocky Road to Kansas. Later the westward movement produced Cactus Flower, Cowboy's Star, and Roads to California.

In these early days the Bible was often the only book in the house, and quilt names show it was well read. Religious women named their designs after Jacob's Ladder, Star of Bethlehem, Joseph's Coat and King David's Crown.

Like folksongs, quilt names evolved from place to place and from generation to generation. Cape Cod's Ship's Wheel became The Harvest Sun in Pennsylvania.

Some of the most colorful pattern names express early lifestyles in a nutshell. Consider Old Maid's Puzzle, Churn Dash, The Reel, or Melon Patch.

Extra care had to be taken in stitching quilts because of an English superstition that twisted or broken threads foretold disaster. While this tradition dictated perfection, another demanded imperfection. For some, flawless work was an affront to God. Consequently, quilts appeared with intentional imperfections.

Superstition influenced not only the mechanics of quilting but also the design itself. Quilts displayed symbols as venerable as the Tree of Life. The language of flowers was the same on a quilt as in a nosegay — red roses for love, lilies for purity, and daisies for innocence. A very ancient symbol, the swastika, meant fertility and good fortune. Pineapples were lucky and brought friends closer together.

Doves were then, as they are now, versatile motifs. They could be used as signs of peace, love, or innocence. Formerly, doves meant femininity, too — our "hen" party used to be called a "dove" party.

A certain pattern called Wandering Foot supposedly compelled boys to roam far from home. When renamed Turkey Tracks, the same pattern was rendered harmless.

Naturally, needleworkers like to have their efforts recognized. Early quilters piled their very best quilts on a guest bed so their visitors would be sure to notice them all. And there were many to see — special quilts for changing seasons, friendships, celebrating marriage — all with their traditions. Many stories are told about quilts as a group, but each individual quilt has its own things to say about history, economics, religion — and about its own creator.

A Colorful Array of Quilting and Patchwork

Though many people visualize quilting and patchwork in the form of bed quilts, don't forget that as techniques they are adaptable to many forms. There's a whole world of ideas in the next few pages just waiting to be explored and expanded, and some of them are right here for you to see, at the left and below. Try our projects, then branch out on your own and use their basic designs or concepts to create something unique.

Several pointers will add that extra bit of ease and enjoyment to your work by preventing misunderstandings or accidental omissions. Initially, your reaction may well be a spontaneous "Oh, I'd like to make that."

Good. Don't make something you won't enjoy doing. But first, read over the directions thoroughly until you can visualize how the item is constructed. Then check what materials are needed. If you do this, you'll never discover half-way through the project that some vital information has been forgotten. If you are a little hazy on techniques, turn to the pages referred to in the text as sources of information.

You'll find toys, clothing, hostess items, home decor, even sports accessories in this chapter for you to make and enjoy. Remember, the sky's the limit for your creative ideas, so take off and sew!

Tree Nap Mat

For nursery school or nap time, what could be more fun than a leafy green tree to curl up on? A suggestion: personalize each child's tree by adding objects he likes.

Materials: 2 yards green fabric, 1 yard brown fabric, ¼ yard blue fabric, ¼ yard each red and yellow prints, all 45″ wide, 1⅔ yards dacron batting over 36″ wide, and thread in black, brown, green, and blue to match yardage.

Add ¼″ seam allowance to *all* pattern pieces.

1. Enlarge patterns to size desired and make brown paper patterns of treetop, trunk, and sky areas between branches. Make a cardboard pattern of the leaf.
2. Trace 36 leaves, 18 in a red print and 18 in a yellow print; add seam allowance and cut out.
3. With right sides of fabric facing, trace, mark, and cut two of each large pattern piece: 2 trunks from brown, 2 treetops from green, 2 sky areas *for each* opening between the branches. Mark top pieces *front* and bottom pieces *back*.
4. Clip and turn edges of sky areas; pin into place on front trunk and topstitch. Attach to back trunk in the same manner.
5. Clip and turn edges of leaves; pin into place on front treetop and zig-zag into place. Try to spread colors evenly throughout treetop.
6. Right side up, lay front tree trunk out flat and place front tree top right side up at the top of the tree trunk. Mark where scallops on lower edge of treetop fall on the trunk and where sides of trunk hit the top of the tree.
7. Clip seams on front treetop, turn, and pin along scallop marks on the trunk. Topstitch twice along this edge to join the two pieces. Carefully join back pieces at the same place in the same manner.
8. Place front and back of tree together with right sides facing and lay a sheet of batting cut to the shape of the tree over the top. Pin the three layers together, turn them over so the batting is on the bottom, then sew around the tree, leaving an opening at the base of the trunk.
9. Trim off the batting outside of seam lines, clip seam allowance and curves at 1″ intervals, and turn the tree rightside out. Blindstitch the base of the trunk closed. Steam everything smooth by holding an iron *above* the surface of the piece.
10. Pin all three layers together thoroughly and quilt by hand or machine around leaves and in parallel lines up and down the trunk to simulate bark.

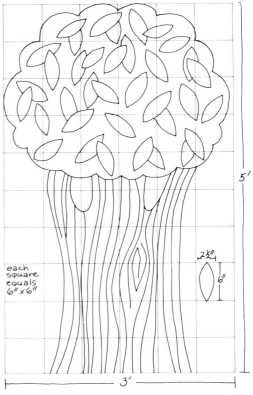

each square equals 6″ x 6″

5′

2½″

6″

3′

Quilted and appliqued tree *is easy to make, a perfect spot for reading a book, napping, or daydreaming.*

Ote-dama Bags

illustration 1.
(step 2)

Ⓑ

Ⓐ

I←3/16" opening

1/4" seam

illustration 2
(step 3)

Ⓑ

Ⓐ

Ⓐ

Ⓑ

see detail, lower left

detail of center seam

H

G

F

Ⓑ

H

G

E

Ⓐ

I

E

F

leave open to turn bag

Ⓐ

Ⓑ

C

D

illustration 3
(step 4)
join corresponding letters to complete

I

C

D

A Japanese toy *with many faces, the ote-dama can be a bean bag, paperweight, or pincushion, depending on your whim.*

What would you like—a bean bag, pincushion, paperweight, or a bibelot? This Japanese plaything can change character at your will, depending on what you put inside. Rice or birdseed are safe fillers for bean bags, sand for the pincushion, and bird grit for paperweights or decorative use.

Materials: ¼ yard each of two contrasting colors, each 45″ wide, thread, rice, sand, or bird grit for filling. (These make inexpensive gifts because 22 bags can be made from ½ yard of material.)

1. Make a cardboard pattern for a rectangle measuring 2″ x 4⅜″. Using this pattern, mark and cut two rectangles out of each color.
2. Lay color A across color B, right sides facing, and sew a ¼″ seam as shown in illustration 1, leaving 3/16″ open at the ends of the seam. Sew the second pair in the same way.
3. Following illustration 2, join pairs to each other, right sides facing, from A to B. See details for seam construction.
4. Carefully following illustration 3, join edges with corresponding letters, always leaving 3/16″ at the end of the seam. Sew up all sides but the last, turn the bag right side out, fill, and slipstitch shut.

Patty Patchwork Doll

(For color photo see facing page)

Cuddly and durable, this muslin doll is sturdy enough to survive the ardent affections of any small child.

Materials: ¼ yard each of green, yellow, red, and blue printed materials 45″ wide, ⅔ yard heavy muslin, ½ yard brown knit material, white, brown, and red thread, loose dacron batting, and embroidery floss in light brown, rose, and pink for doll's face.

Add ¼″ seam allowance to *all* pattern pieces.

1. Enlarge the pattern of the doll to the correct size and make a brown paper pattern.
2. Make a 1½″ square cardboard pattern for patches.
3. Cut 22 squares of yellow print, 22 from the blue print, 22 from the red print, and 22 from the green.
4. Make two lengths of patchwork fabric by sewing the squares together, first in rows, then into complete pieces, following the color key in diagram 1. The colors should run diagonally. Two squares will be left over for the doll's feet.
5. Cut two doll bodies from the muslin.
6. Trace on and embroider doll's face. The features may be transferred to the muslin by punching through the pattern onto the muslin with a sharp pencil, leaving dots outlining the areas to be embroidered.

7. Lay patchwork material right side up over the doll's body, positioning it to cover the muslin from the neck to the legs and halfway down the arms.
8. Turn under raw edges along skirt hem, around neck, across arms, and on doll's toes and topstitch the dress into place on the front of the doll. Follow the same steps for attaching a dress to the doll's back.
9. Right sides facing, pin and sew together the two halves of the doll, being sure to catch the raw edges of the dress. Start at one shoulder with a ¼″ seam and sew around to the opposite shoulder, leaving tops of shoulders and head open.
10. Trim seams to ⅛″, clip curves every ¾″, turn, and press with a warm iron.
11. Stuff the doll with loose dacron batting, then turn in the seams and slipstitch the opening closed.
12. Cut ½″ x 24″ strips of brown knit fabric, pleat them into ¼″ folds, thread onto buttonhole twist, and tie to hold pleats (illustration 1). Tack onto doll's head in a spiral from center out to make hair, as shown below (illustration 2).

A suggestion: instead of a patchwork dress for our doll, how about using plain fabric with an applique design?

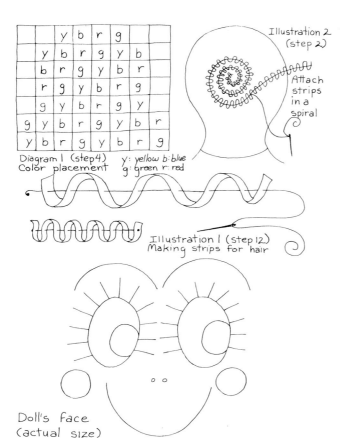

	y	b	r	g		
y	b	r	g	y	b	
b	r	g	y	b	r	
r	g	y	b	r	g	
g	y	b	r	g	y	
g	y	b	r	g	y	b
y	b	r	g	y	b	r	g

Diagram I (step 4)
Color placement   y: yellow b: blue
g: green r: red

Illustration 2 (step 2)
Attach strips in a spiral

Illustration I (step 12)
Making strips for hair

Doll's face (actual size)

Each square = 2½″ x 2½″

Soft Building Blocks

Stuffed building blocks are safe, soft, washable, and easy for little hands to grasp. Our designs on the following page may be used, or pictures may be traced from your child's favorite coloring book. A suggestion: enlarge our designs to 12″ squares for quilt blocks.

Materials: ¼ yard 45″ wide fabric of each color to be used (colors are indicated on each design), matching thread, black thread, and embroidery floss for small details.

Add ¼″ seam allowance to all pattern pieces.

1. Enlarge designs to the proper size.
2. Cut two 4″ squares from typing paper for each block. Centering the design properly, trace it onto both squares, using one for pattern pieces and one to make a stencil for drawing the design onto the background block. Transfer all colors and numbers from the design into the proper places on the squares.
3. Ignoring the broken outline around the design (this indicates a stitched outline to be done when all pieces are appliqued into place), cut out each pattern piece from one design. On the second paper square, carefully cut away the pattern areas with a razor blade to make a stencil. This will be used to transfer the de-sign onto the background square by tracing.
4. Cut a 4½″ square from the desired background color. Lay the stencil over this fabric square, centering carefully, and, with a sharp pencil, trace on the design. Draw slightly inside of the cut out areas so pencil marks won't show later on.
5. Trace applique patterns onto right sides of proper colors, adding seam allowances, and cut out each piece. Clipping curves and angles almost to the pencil lines, turn under seam allowances and iron flat.
6. Pin applique pieces into place over the pencil lines drawn on the background squares and sew, using an invisible stitch, as shown on page 23. Such details as faces are embroidered with French knots, backstitch, or satin stitch, as shown below.
7. When all pieces are attached, outline design with black thread in a running stitch, as shown on page 23.
8. Each building block contains four appliqued sides and two plain. Following illustration 1, join the six sides, leaving ¼″ open at the end of each seam. Construct block by matching sides with corresponding letters, again leaving ¼″ open at the end of each seam. Sew down remaining square as shown in illustration 2.
9. Turn, stuff with dacron batting, and sew shut by hand.

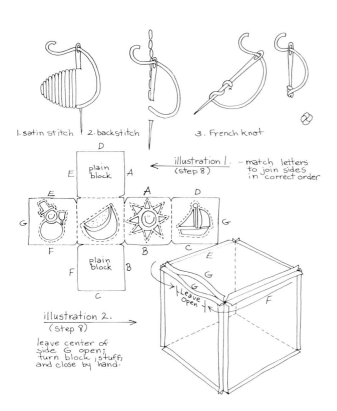

Directions for Patty Patchwork are on facing page; applique building blocks are soft, washable playthings for baby.

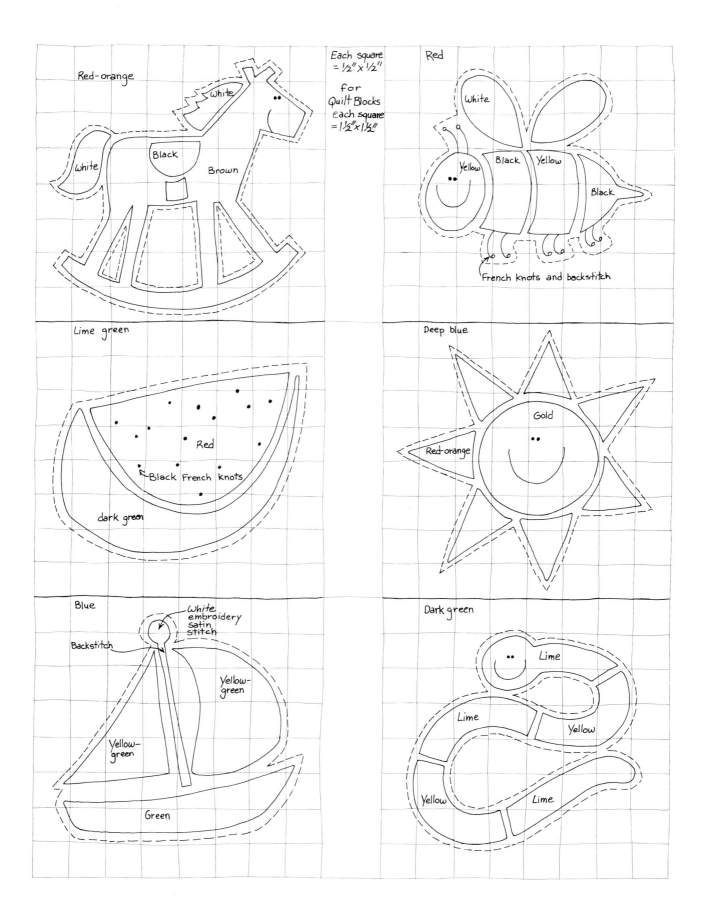

Red-orange

White

White

Black

Brown

Each square
= ½" x ½"

for
Quilt Blocks
each square
= 1½" x 1½"

Red

White

Yellow

Black

Yellow

Black

French knots and backstitch

Lime green

Red

Black French knots

dark green

Deep blue

Gold

Red-orange

Blue

White
embroidery
satin
stitch

Backstitch

Yellow-
green

Yellow-
green

Green

Dark green

Lime

Lime

Yellow

Yellow

Lime

Patchwork Placemats

(For color photo see page 42)

This set of four placemats in a variety of prints is inexpensive and easy to make, for each mat is just a mix and match copy of the others.

Materials: ⅓ yard each of four 45″ wide complementary colored print fabrics, 1 yard of 45″ wide lining fabric, and thread.

Add ¼″ for seam allowance to *all* pattern pieces.

1. Draw a 13″ square on lightweight cardboard.
2. Find the centers of each side (6½″), mark, and connect to make a second square.
3. Find the centers for the sides of the second square (4½″), mark, and connect to form a third square.
4. Mark the centers of the third square (3¼″) and connect the dots to form the fourth and final square.
5. Number each piece as shown in the diagram below and cut apart to make individual patterns.
6. Trace one of each pattern piece onto each of the four print fabrics, being sure to add seam allowance.
7. Cut out each piece and place them in numerical order (some pattern pieces may look the same, but there are small differences which will affect the pieces when they are sewn together). When finished, you will have four placemat groups, each laid out by color with the pattern pieces in numerical order.

8. Cut two 3½″ x 13½″ strips from each print fabric and lay them next to the pieces with the same matching printed design.
9. Move all center squares and strips over to the next group, all triangles for the second square over two groups, all triangles for the third square over three groups, and leave triangles for the fourth outside square where they are. This will give an even mixture of prints throughout all placemats (see illustration 1).
10. Using a ¼″ seam, sew all pieces together in numerical order from the center out.
11. Press all seams flat, not open, with a warm iron.
12. Cut the lining material into four pieces the same size as each placemat.
13. Place the lining material and placemats with their right sides facing. Pin into place and sew up around three sides completely. From both corners, sew in 7 inches on the fourth side, leaving a 5-inch-wide opening at the center.
14. Trim excess cloth from all corners and turn the placemats right side out.
15. Press placemats again, especially along the edges, and slipstitch the opening closed by hand (see page 23 for stitch diagram).

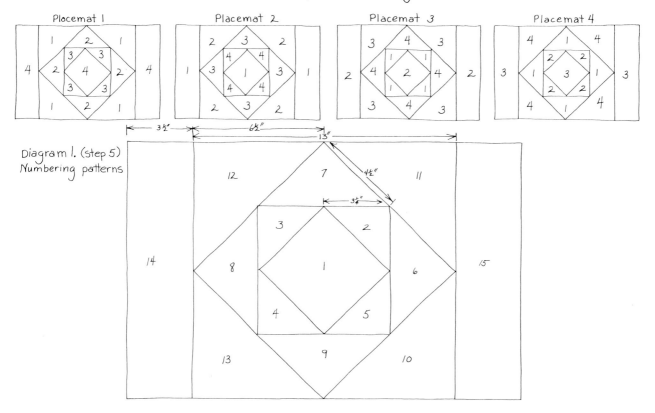

Illustration 1. (step 9)   Color organization

Diagram 1. (step 5) Numbering patterns

Hostess Apron and Hot Pads

Entertaining can be great fun, especially if the mood is gay and glamorous. Add some glamour of your own in our long-stemmed hostess apron, designed to protect you beautifully from kitchen to canapé table. Use the accompanying hot pad for a warm serving platter, steaming vegetables, or a hot hors d'oeuvres tray.

Materials: 1¾ yards 45″ wide fabric in light green, 1¾ yards 45″ wide matching lining, ½ yard each of dark pink and light pink, ¾ yard of dark green, ¼ yard of Velcro fastening tape, 1 package of deep pink seam binding, thread of each color, and loose batting.

Add ¼″ seam allowance to *all* pattern pieces.

1. Measure from waist to ankle and around waist.
2. Cut one yard of 45″ wide light green fabric in half crosswise, making two lengths each 45″ long and 18″ wide. Cut lining fabric, following same directions.
3. Right sides facing, sew lining lengths to fabric lengths on the two 45″ sides to make two skirt lengths.

4. Turn skirts to right sides and gather one 18″ side of each to fit ½ of the waist measurement minus 2″. Fold gathered edges to find centers and mark them with a pin. Set skirts aside until step 13.
5. Cut two squares of fabric for apron bibs measuring ½ of waist measurement minus 2″ for all sides. Following same directions, cut lining material to match.
6. Enlarge the rose pattern to the correct size and trace onto tissue paper. Transfer the design from tissue paper to one of the fabric squares.
7. Trace and cut out pattern pieces for applique.
8. Using the general techniques for applique found on pages 21 to 23 and the directions for stuffed applique on page 29, work the pieces as numbered for ease in fitting the design together. Add finishing touches with pink embroidery floss if desired.
9. Right sides facing, sew lining and bib together on two opposite *sides*. Leaving 2 inches open at each end, sew the top raw edges closed; turn and press.
10. Fold bottom edges of bibs to find centers and mark with a straight pin.

Brightly cheerful, *patchwork placemats are machine washable, quickly and economically made (directions on page 41).*

An American beauty apron, *this rose-adorned coverup is just right for parties or special entertaining.*

11. Cut four rectangles for waistbands from dark green, each 3" wide by ½ the waist measurement plus 3" long.

12. Right sides facing, sew together each pair of rectangles on the short ends; fold crosswise to find centers and mark with pins.

13. Match centers of gathered skirt edges and bib edges to centers of waistbands; mark where outside edges of skirts and bibs fall on the edges of waistbands.

14. Remove both skirts and bibs from waistbands; sew from end seams of waistbands in along seam lines to marks where outside edges of skirts and bibs fall. Clip corners and turn. (See illustration 1.)

15. Cut two strips of fabric each 2" x 30" (add ¼" seam allowance to all sides). Double each over into 15" lengths and sew longest sides to make straps; turn.

16. Insert 2" straps into 2" openings in the plain bib at a slight outward angle. Pin and hand sew to secure.

17. Insert edges of bibs into waistbands and pin. Do the same for gathered edges of skirts. Topstitch ⅛" deep entirely around waistbands to secure both pieces.

18. Pin shoulder straps to openings in front bib and put apron on; adjust straps to fit shoulders and re-pin. Remove apron and sew straps as in step 16.

19. Cut two pieces of Velcro fastening tape, each 2" long, and separate into four pieces. Put apron on and adjust waistband to fit; mark where front overlap falls on back waistband. Remove apron and sew Velcro strip on inside of front waistband ends. Sew second strip to marks on outside of back waistband.

20. Put apron on and measure hem. Measure up about 2½ inches from hemline and mark.

21. Enlarge leaf pattern to desired size, trace onto tissue paper and then along marked line on the skirt.

22. Trace and cut leaves from dark green fabric and make stems from a bias cut strip. Applique into place as you did with rose on apron bib, being careful not to catch the lining material. Press with a warm iron.

23. Turn edges of lining and fabric to inside at hemline. Pin seam and blindstitch hem into place. Press.

Hot pads

1. Cut four squares of light green each 8½" x 8½".

2. Following directions in steps 6 through 8 for apron, and omitting the stuffing procedure, cut out and applique roses to two of the squares.

3. Cut an 8½" x 8½" square from an old mattress pad or cotton batting. Avoid dacron; it conducts heat.

4. Place a plain square and an appliqued square right sides facing on top of the padding square and pin. Seam on three sides; turn and press (illustration 2).

5. Baste layers together with pins or large stitches and quilt the rose along seam lines. Quilt remainder of hot pad by following outline of rose, keeping rows of stitching ¼" apart. Edge hot pad with bias tape.

A suggestion: not partial to roses? Try another design or another color. Shorten the apron if you wish or make a tunic top or a dressy jumper to wear over slacks.

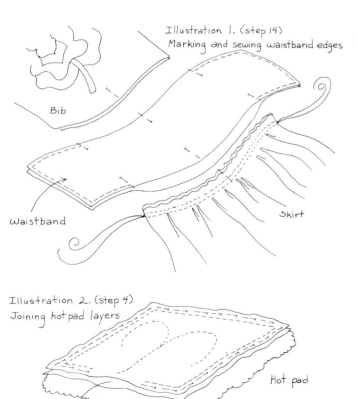

Illustration 1. (step 14)
Marking and sewing waistband edges

Bib

Waistband

Skirt

Illustration 2. (step 4)
Joining hot pad layers

Hot pad

Turn
right side out

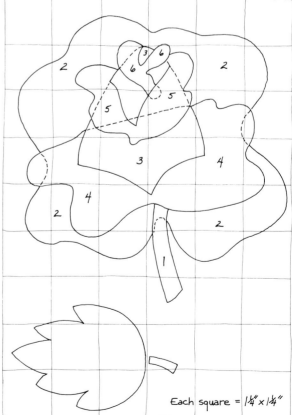

Each square = 1¼" x 1¼"

Hand-Painted and Quilted Vest

A lighthearted approach to showing your true colors, this vest will cheer up even the gloomiest of days.

Materials: 2 yards heavy unbleached muslin, white thread, black thread, loose dacron batting, red, blue, yellow, green, and purple textile paints, and brushes.

Add ¼″ seam allowance to *all* pattern pieces.

1. Wash and dry muslin to shrink and remove sizing.
2. Measure: waist, 5″ up from waist; top of shoulder to 5″ up from waist, front and back; neck to shoulder.
3. Enlarge pattern pieces and designs to proper size and adjust to suit your measurements: lengthen or shorten, adjust bust darts and slant of shoulders.
4. Lay out patterns on muslin and pin into place.
5. Add seam allowances to all pieces and cut out as many pieces as indicated on patterns.
6. Sew front waistbands to back waistbands.
7. Tape tissue patterns to a window, align pattern pieces to seam markings on tissue, tape down, and trace design onto *unmarked* sides of pattern pieces with a pencil. Trace designs onto only *one* set of vest patterns.
8. To paint, lay out individual pieces on masonite board or any non-porous flat surface. Thin paints with water and test on a scrap of muslin before starting. Apply colors quickly, then allow to dry overnight. Press.
9. Sew darts on painted bodices and, with right sides facing, seam to painted back at shoulders.
10. Right sides facing, seam painted waistband to plain waistband on bottom and sides. Clip corners and turn. Iron under seam allowance along top raw edge.
11. Sew bust darts, then join plain bodices to plain back at shoulders.
12. Sew painted pieces to plain pieces along outer and inner edges, leaving bottoms of back and bodices free.
13. Turn vest and press. Insert bottom edge of vest back into turned upper edge of back waistband, then pin. Pin raw edges of bodices into front waistbands.
14. Topstitch along turned edge of waistband.
15. By either hand or machine, sew with small stitches along outlines of areas to be stuffed. For detailed directions on stuffing, see pages 28-29.
16. Turn vest inside out; inside of outlined area cut a slit through lining, stuff lightly with loose dacron batt, and sew slit shut with overcast stitches.

A suggestion: use this vest pattern as a vehicle to create your own personal statement. How about painting your astrological sign — or a field of flowers?

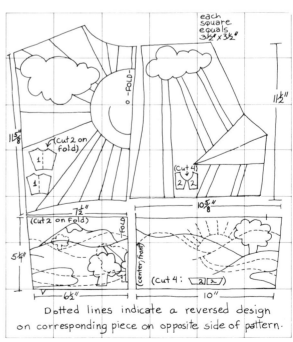

Hand painted muslin vest *embellished with English padding sports a smiling sun and storybook landscape.*

Crazy Patch Skirt/Comforter

Simple to make, yet visually smashing, our long wrap-around skirt can accurately be termed a "designer original" . . . designed and originated by you! Should your tastes change, transform your skirt into a child-size tied comforter in a jiffy.

Materials: sewing scraps or a variety of yardage in a pleasing color combination (ours happens to be autumn colors), 1¾ yards 45″ wide lining material in a compatible color, thread complementary to your color scheme, 2½ yards 1½″ wide grosgrain ribbon (preshrunk), and 4″ of Velcro fastening tape. Keep the same fabric type throughout the skirt.

1. Cut your fabrics into a variety of shapes and sizes, trying not to make them too small.
2. Following the directions for machine zigzag crazy patch on page 19, begin to sew the patches at one corner of the large rectangle of lining fabric. One at a time, sew the patches by slightly overlapping edges and sewing them with a narrow zigzag stitch. Spread prints and solids evenly throughout the skirt.
3. When the entire rectangle is covered with patches, pleat one 63″ side into large, flat pleats. Space them to fall on either side of center front for a more flatter-ing line. When the pleated edge measures about 40″, pin the pleats in place.
4. Finish the sides of the skirt by folding over a 1″ hem, pinning it, and hemstitching into place.
5. Fold ribbon in half and crease. Starting at one corner of pleated edge, pin, then sew ribbon from end A to end B, fold the ribbon around B to the front of the skirt and topstitch back to end A as shown in illustration 1. Fold under the raw edge of the ribbon at A and stitch closed. Sew along top edges of ribbon to join, as shown in illustration 2.
6. Try on the skirt and mark where the overlap falls in the back. Position the Velcro strips and sew them into place, half on the overlap and half on the skirt.
7. Hem bottom edge of skirt and press out any wrinkles with a steam iron.

Tied comforter

Remove waistband and pleats from skirt. Press out creases. Put together skirt and backing material with right sides facing and lay over a rectangle of dacron batting. Sew the three layers together on three sides, turning and sewing fourth side closed by hand. Pin and tie, following directions on page 28.

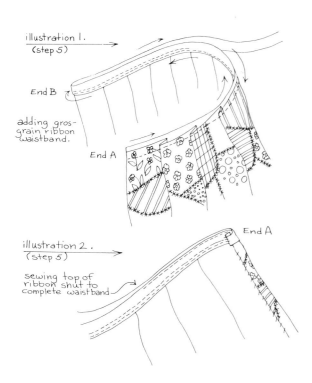

illustration 1.
(step 5)

End B

adding grosgrain ribbon waistband.

End A

End A

illustration 2.
(step 5)

sewing top of ribbon shut to complete waistband

Skirt of many colors *leads a double life; when you've finished wearing it convert it into a tied crazy patch comforter.*

Patchwork Tie

(For color photo see facing page)

That familiar long, flat, rectangular gift box will open to reveal something very special if it contains a hand-made patchwork tie. Personalize his gift by including his favorite colors or motifs.

Materials: scraps of cottons, silks, or synthetic blends in coordinated colors (avoid heavy or loosely woven fabrics), ½ yard 36″ wide lightweight interfacing, ⅓ yard 36″ wide facing material (similar to that used in the tie), and matching thread.

Add ¼″ seam allowance to *all* pattern pieces.

1. Cut scraps into squares, rectangles, trapezoids, or right-angle triangles, keeping them small and approximately the same size.
2. Assemble these patches in 30″ long strips, making sure the fabric grains of the patches all go in the same direction and that colors are randomly spread throughout the strip (illustration 1).
3. Continue to make strips of patches and sew the strips together until the entire patchwork measures 30″ x 36″. Press the seams open (illustration 2).
4. Enlarge the tie patterns to the proper size, trace the patterns for both interfacings and both facings onto tissue paper, and then cut out all patterns. (Interfac-

ings are marked with diagonal lines, whereas facings are indicated by vertical lines.)

5. Lay front and back tie patterns *diagonally* (on the bias) on the patchwork rectangle, pin, and cut out, remembering to add seam allowance.
6. Lay interfacing patterns on the bias of interfacing fabric and facing patterns on the bias of facing fabric. Pin and cut out.
7. Right sides facing, sew tie front to tie back on diagonal center seam. Sew front interfacing to back interfacing in same manner. Lay tie and interfacing face down and press seams open.
8. Lay interfacing along dotted lines on wrong side of tie. Tack into place on patchwork seams.
9. Right sides facing, sew front facing to tie front and back facing to tie back. Clip corners, turn right sides out, and press lightly.
10. Fold tie to back along broken lines (illustration 3). Turn under raw edges and slipstitch into place. Applique may be used to cover up problem areas, if any, or to personalize the tie by adding a special design or pattern.

A suggestion: instead of using randomly shaped patches, why not create a bold diagonally striped fabric for your tie?

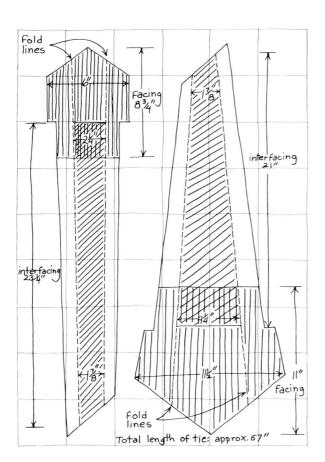

Illustration 1. (step 2) Sew patches into strips

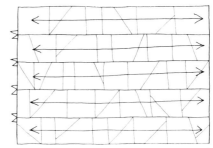

Illustration 2. (step 3) Sew strips together

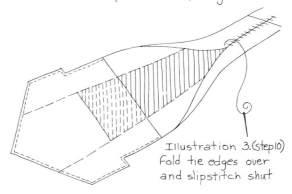

Illustration 3. (step 10) Fold tie edges over and slipstitch shut

Ohio Star Tote Bag

Shown on our cover, a traditional Ohio Star shoulder bag can be put to many uses. Carry your own essentials, baby's necessities, or small purchases in this durable, machine washable tote. (Note: the construction of our purse utilizes a method commonly used for joining conventional quilt blocks. See pages 17 and 18.)

Materials: 1⅛ yards 45″ wide blue material, ¼ yard 45″ wide yellow print material, 22″ x 45″ length of dacron batt, and matching threads.

Add ¼″ seam allowance to *all* pattern pieces.

1. Cut out a 12″ square piece of paper. Measure or fold the square into nine smaller squares, each 4″ x 4″. Then fold AD, CF, EH, and GB to complete design (illustration 1).

2. Open folded square out flat and make a cardboard pattern of one triangle and of one square. Remember to add seam allowance to all edges.

3. Make patterns for: two joining strips, 4″ x 12½″; two shoulder straps and two strap linings, each 4″ x 29½″; and one purse lining, 12½″ x 43½″.

4. Mark and cut out all pattern pieces very accurately to assure proper fit when joining.

5. Matching corners carefully (as in illustration 2), join triangles to form a block (a), join blocks into a row (b), and rows into a square (c). Press seams flat.

6. When the three blocks are completed, join blocks with strips as shown in illustration 3.

7. Lay a 13″ x 44″ rectangle of batting on a sheet of newspaper. Place joined blocks face up over batting, then place lining right side *down* over joined blocks.

8. Pin all edges, then machine stitch along seam around the rectangle, leaving a 6″ opening in the middle of one short edge. Tear off paper, trim corners, turn, and adjust corners. Stitch closed.

9. Right sides facing, join shoulder strap pieces to one another on one short end. Do same for lining. Cut a length of batt slightly larger than the shoulder strap from remaining dacron batt.

10. Pin batt, strap, and lining together as in step 7.

11. Sew both long sides, leaving ends open. Tear off paper, turn straps, and sew ends closed by hand turning under the raw edges.

12. Purse is quilted by stitching as close as possible to the seams on the blocks. Quilt joining strips and shoulder straps, as shown in illustration 4.

13. Join shoulder strap (lining sides together) to purse sides and bottom by topstitching ⅜″ in from edge (illustration 4).

ALYSON SMITH GONSALVES/ANNE MITCHELL

Patchwork tie *makes one-of-a-kind gift (directions on facing page); Ohio Star tote bag can be put to a variety of uses.*

Crazy Patch Racquet Cover

(For color photo see page 50)

The wear and tear of hanging around the courts won't faze this durable tennis racquet cover. Tough corduroy scraps are combined by machine zig-zag to create a washable surface that can withstand rough use. A Velcro closure makes construction simple.

Materials: ½ yard 45" wide heavy muslin, corduroy scraps in red, black, and green, 1 package of red double fold bias tape, 1 spool of black thread and 1 yard Velcro tape.

Add ¼" seam allowance to *all* pattern pieces.

1. Lay the tennis racquet to be covered on a sheet of heavy paper. (Note: use only the racquet you intend to cover since there are many racquet sizes and shapes. Two racquets may look the same but be different.)
2. Trace around the head of the racquet and down the neck 3" on each side to create a pattern for the racquet cover.
3. Measuring carefully with a ruler, add 1" to all sides of the pattern to account for the width of the racquet and the seams (see illustration 1).
4. Cut out the pattern, keeping curved edges as smooth and true as possible.
5. Lay pattern on heavy muslin, pin, and trace two patterns. *Do not* cut out at this time.
6. Cut corduroy scraps in random shapes of medium size. Lay out the scraps over the uncut muslin patterns and shuffle around until the color combination is balanced. Pin the scraps into place, slightly overlapping the edges. Machine zigzag over raw edges to secure scraps to muslin. Be sure that edges of scraps slightly overlap seamlines so that all edges will be covered when pattern pieces are sewn together (illustration 2).
7. When all scraps are sewn down, carefully cut out pattern pieces, being sure to cut them exactly the same.
8. Baste one continuous length of bias tape all around the edges of *each* pattern piece, then sew into place by topstitching (illustration 3).
9. Lay head of racquet at the neck to determine how wide the neck opening should be to allow the racquet to be inserted or removed from the cover. Mark these points as shown in illustration 4.
10. With *wrong* sides facing, pin both pattern pieces together and join by sewing from one mark to the other around head of racquet cover.
11. Sew strips of Velcro to edges of neck openings. Sew by machine on bias tape edge and by hand on inside edge. On curves, Velcro may have to be clipped (illustration 5).

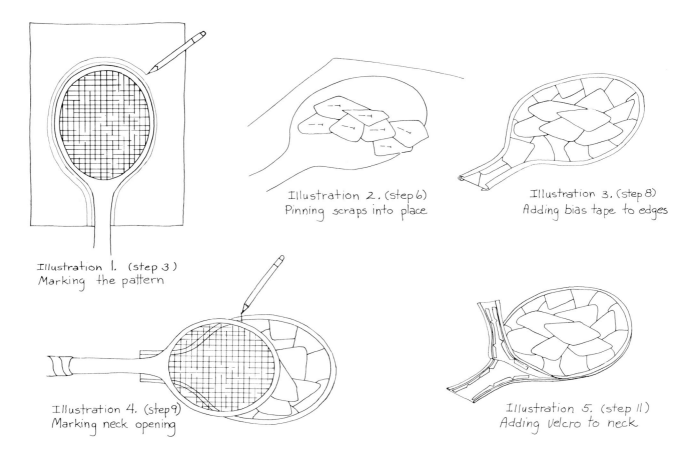

Illustration 1. (step 3)
Marking the pattern

Illustration 2. (step 6)
Pinning scraps into place

Illustration 3. (step 8)
Adding bias tape to edges

Illustration 4. (step 9)
Marking neck opening

Illustration 5. (step 11)
Adding Velcro to neck

"Fat Towel" Poolside Mat

(For color photo see page 50)

Soft, comfortable poolside sitting can easily be arranged if our "Fat Towel" is in residence. Made from plushy velour bath towels, this poolside mat can soften the hard, rough touch of concrete or brick.

Materials: 4 red velour bath size towels, approximately 24″ x 43″, 2¾ yards 45″ wide blue lightweight duck for backing, 45″ x 97″ roll of dacron batt, red heavy-duty thread.

Use selvages of towels for seam allowances.

1. Place two towels together with right sides (velour sides) facing. Carefully line up all edges, then pin or baste along one long edge.
2. Using the selvage along this edge as a seam allowance, sew up the edge as close as possible to the point where the selvage stops and the velour begins. This will make the upper surface of the finished mat appear to be one continuous length of velour.
3. Take two remaining towels, join as explained in steps 1 and 2. When the two pairs of towels are made up, place them together with right sides facing (illustration 1) and join on long sides to make one continuous length.
4. Velour side down, lay the mat out on a large, flat surface. Place dacron batt over mat and trim it to a size slightly larger than the mat.
5. Place rectangle of batting on a flat surface, lay mat over batt, with velour side *up,* then place blue backing material, right side *down,* over mat (illustration 2). Pin all edges together through all three layers.
6. Trim batt and backing even with the edges of the mat, then machine stitch around the mat, using a ½″ seam allowance. Begin 6″ in on one short side, then stitch down one long side and around one short end, up the second long side, and 6″ in on the fourth side, leaving a 12″ opening in the center of this side.
7. Trim corners, turn right sides out, push corners out into points, then handstitch opening closed.
8. Enlarge latticework diagram to correct size for quilting pattern (see page 26 on marking for quilting), measure, mark, and connect 3″ intervals (as shown in diagram) on backing with tailor's chalk or pastel pencil.
9. Pin or baste layers of material every few inches to hold in place while piece is being quilted, then roll mat up tightly from one short end to the center.
10. Place the roll under the arm of the sewing machine and quilt in straight lines from center to outside edge, skipping appropriate sections for lattice pattern and unrolling the mat as you go. Repeat for rest of mat.

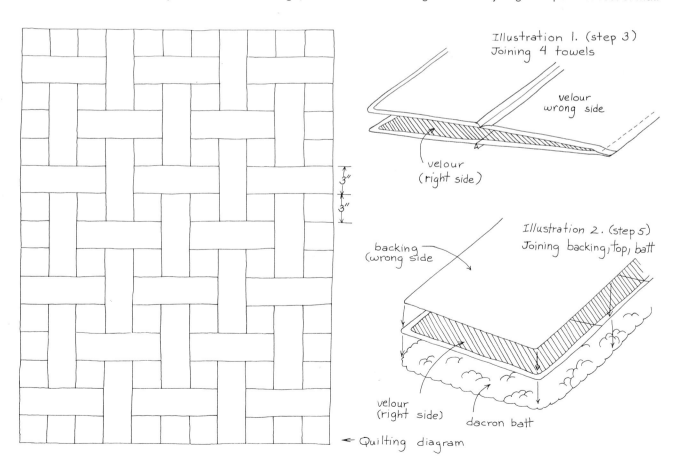

Illustration 1. (step 3)
Joining 4 towels

velour wrong side

velour (right side)

3″
3″

Illustration 2. (step 5)
Joining backing, top, batt

backing (wrong side)

velour (right side)

dacron batt

← Quilting diagram

Quilted velour towels *(upper left) create comfortable mat for pool or beach use (directions on page 49). Crazy patch racquet cover (lower left) is made of machine-sewn corduroy scraps (for directions, see page 48). Parsons tabletop (lower right) sports cheerful patchwork design (directions on facing page).*

Patchwork Parsons Table

(For color photo see facing page)

Walls, chairs, tables, even floors — all flat surfaces are fair game for paste-on patchwork. One example is our Parsons table topped off with a traditional quilt block pattern: Robbing Peter to Pay Paul.

Materials: 1 wooden parson's table 18″ x 18″ x 15″, ½ yard each 45″ wide blue printed fabric and plain gold fabric, white glue, 1″ wide inexpensive paint brush, enamel undercoat, ½ pint deep blue gloss enamel paint, thinner, 1½″ wide paint brush, and shellac or clear plastic spray.

1. Cut 18″ x 18″ square from cardboard and trace patchwork design onto the square. Number all pieces as shown in illustration 1.
2. Cut design apart carefully, using a straightedge and razorblade or art knife for greater accuracy.
3. Trace striped patterns of diagram onto the wrong side of the blue printed material and trace plain patterns onto the wrong side of the gold fabric.
4. Trace pattern, piece by piece in numerical order, onto the top of the parson's table. This will give a pattern to follow when gluing down the fabric pieces (illustration 2).
5. Cut patterns from fabric, being extremely accurate when cutting edges so they will match when glued down.
6. Mix white glue with water to a consistency like heavy milk (make about ¾ cup) and begin to brush glue onto top of parson's table, covering only striped areas in one row (example: brush glue on areas 1, 3, 5, 6, 8, and 10 in first row only). Use an inexpensive brush.
7. Allow glue to become tacky, then apply fabric pieces to the proper areas and smooth into place.
8. Do the same for the remaining 5 rows.
9. When all pieces of one color are applied, allow them to dry thoroughly before applying the second color.
10. Add the second color pattern pieces in the same manner, allowing them to dry completely.
11. When the top of the table is completely dry, trim off excess fabric or rough edges from the edges of the pattern pieces, using a sharp art knife or razor blade. Remove by rubbing over the cut area with a finger and pulling up the excess cloth.
12. Lay out newspaper, turn the table on one side, and paint with enamel undercoat, turning the table on its top to complete the fourth side and legs.
13. When undercoat is dry, apply two coats of blue gloss enamel to sides and legs of table. Shellac table top or spray with clear plastic spray coat to protect fabric from stains or dirt.

Each square = 3″ x 3″

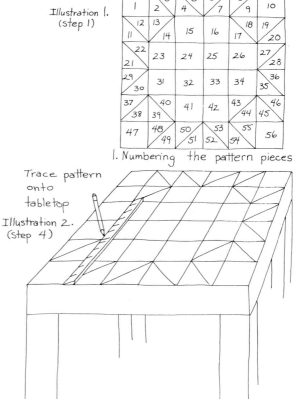

Illustration 1. (step 1)

1. Numbering the pattern pieces

Trace pattern onto tabletop

Illustration 2. (step 4)

Quilted tea towel *can be quickly and inexpensively finished, making a perfect last-minute gift (directions on page 55).*

Dramatic *modular room divider is felt with ancient Aztec design influence (for directions, see pages 56 and 57).*

Super-Graphic *fabric "painting" measures 3' x 3', a bold, modern approach to patchwork (directions on page 54).*

Old-fashioned schoolhouse *goes modern with pink, lavender, and orange patchwork (directions on facing page).*

Little Schoolhouse Pillow

(For color photo see facing page)

Traditionally known as the Little Red Schoolhouse pattern, our pillow has transformed itself into a confection of pastels, framed in pink and playfully tasseled. This little schoolhouse adapts easily to any mood or decor; just change the colors to suit your fancy.

Materials: ½ yard dark pink material; ½ yard unbleached muslin; ¼ yard each of purple print, orange, light pink, and purple fabrics; dark pink thread; pink acrylic yarn; and dacron batting. All fabrics should be 45″ wide.

Add ¼″ seam allowance to *all* pattern pieces.

1. Enlarge pattern pieces to correct size.
2. Trace patterns onto cardboard, number as shown in diagram, and cut apart into individual pieces.
3. Trace, mark, and cut out pattern pieces, remembering to add seam allowances. Cut 1, 3, and 5 from plain purple fabric; cut 2, 4, 8, 10, 17, and 19 from purple print fabric; cut 7, 13, and 14 from orange fabric; cut 6, 9, 11, 12, 15, 16, 18, 20, and 21 from light pink fabric; cut 4 border strips and two 16″ x 10″ rectangles from dark pink fabric. Remember seam allowances.
4. Sew individual pattern pieces together in the following order (illustration 1): 1 to 2 to 3 to 4 to 5 to form section A; sew 7 to 8 to form section B; sew 9 to 10 to 11, add 6 to top, then sew 12 to bottom, forming section C; sew 16 to 17 to 18 to 19 to 20, then add 14 and 15 to top, 13 to the left side, and 21 to bottom to make up section D.
5. Combine all sections into one piece in the following manner: sew section B to C along a; pivot slightly at corner. Sew D to BC along b. Sew D to BC along c, whipstitching by hand. Sew A to sections BCD at d. Sew seams e and f by hand.
6. Press all seams flat, *not* open.
7. Add pink border strips, mitering corners by hand.
8. To make pillow back, sew a narrow hem on one long side of each large pink rectangle. Place pillow front face *up* on table and lay rectangles face *down* over pillow front. Overlap hemmed edges of rectangles until their outside raw edges are even with the edges of the pillow front (illustration 2). Pin together and sew a ¼″ seam around the entire pillow, curving the seam in to ⅜″ at corners. Turn and press.
9. Make a pillow insert from two 17½″ squares of muslin sewn together and stuffed with dacron. Insert into the pillow.
10. Make yarn tassels (illustration 3) and sew to corners.

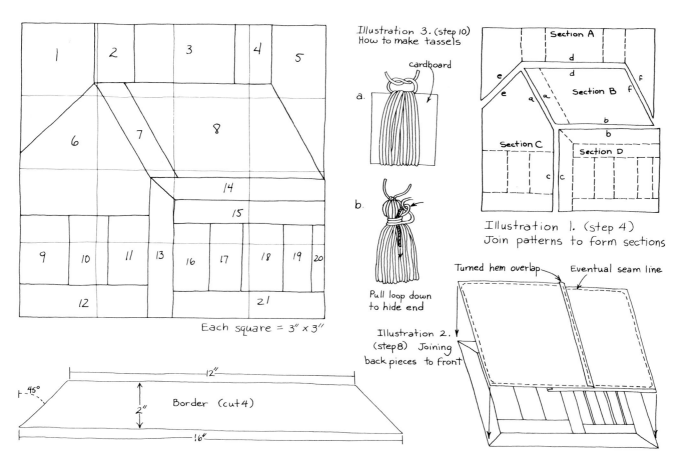

Each square = 3″ x 3″

Border (cut 4)
12″
2″
16″
45°

Illustration 3. (step 10) How to make tassels
cardboard
a.
b.
Pull loop down to hide end

Illustration 1. (step 4) Join patterns to form sections
Section A
Section B
Section C
Section D

Illustration 2. (step 8) Joining back pieces to front
Turned hem overlap
Eventual seam line

Super-Graphic

(For color photo see page 52)

Having undergone a radical personality change, the traditional Beggar's Block pattern steps forth as Super-Graphic, a bold 3' x 3' statement in primary colors. For visual impact, it's hard to beat.

Materials: ½ yard 45" wide white sailcloth; ⅔ yard 45" wide blue sailcloth, ⅓ yard 45" wide red sailcloth, ½ yard 45" wide yellow sailcloth, white thread, four 3' stretcher bars, hammer, staple gun, and staples.

Add ¼" seam allowance to *all* pattern pieces.

1. Using a ruler, draw a 1' x 1' square on heavy cardboard. Be sure to measure corners and sides accurately.
2. Divide the square into horizontal thirds and mark. Each ⅓ will equal 4" wide by 12" long.
3. Draw lines diagonally across the square, skipping over the center ⅓ (illustration 1). Number the pieces of the pattern as shown in illustration 1 and keep to this order when assembling the individual blocks to make squares come out correctly.
4. Cut apart the square and trace the following number of patterns, using the indicated cardboard pieces and leaving room for seam allowances. From blue — 20 triangles: 5 each from #1, #3, #5, and #7, and 8 trapezoids: 4 each from #2 and #6; from red — 4 triangles: 1 each from #1, #3, #5, and #7, and 4 bars, all cut from #4; from white — 8 triangles: 2 each from #1, #2, #3, and #4, and 8 trapezoids: 4 each from #2 and #6; from yellow — 4 bars: all cut from #4, and one 1' x 1' square.

5. Add seam allowances and cut out patterns.
6. Following the large diagram below for color placement, sew individual pattern pieces into strips, then sew the strips together to make a block (illustration 2). Sew blocks together into rows, placing colors as shown in diagram. To match corners accurately, see page 15. Join rows together properly to make a 3' x 3' square.
7. Cut four 37" x 3" strips from remaining blue fabric and attach to all four sides of graphic (illustration 3).
8. Join 4 stretcher bars to make a frame by placing the corners of 2 bars at right angles, preferably against a wall corner, and tapping them together with a hammer until they lock. Repeat for remaining 3 corners and square up the frame (illustration 4).
9. Attach graphic by laying it face down on floor, placing frame over design and adjusting frame edges to design edges. Bring blue strips around to back of frame and staple at centers of frame backs. Work out from these points toward the edges, stretching and stapling as you go.

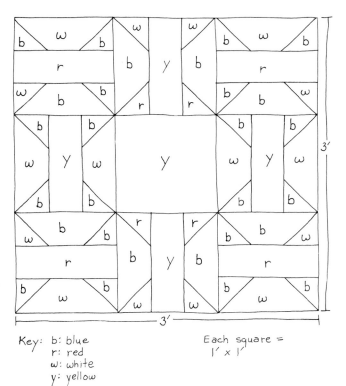

Key: b: blue
       r: red
       w: white
       y: yellow

Each square = 1' x 1'

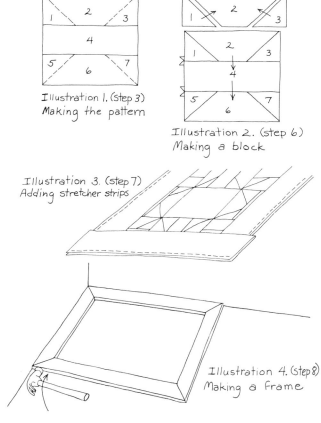

Illustration 1. (step 3)
Making the pattern

Illustration 2. (step 6)
Making a block

Illustration 3. (step 7)
Adding stretcher strips

Illustration 4. (step 8)
Making a frame

Quilted Tea Towel

(For color photo see page 52)

Tea towels have more uses than just drying an occasional dish or wiping hands. Add some dacron batt, take a few quilting stitches, attach two cross bars, and you'll have a very striking wall hanging. A great variety of tea towels is available; subject matter varies from spices or fruits and vegetables to horses, sailing ships, and old Victorian prints; something for just about everyone. And you can probably find designs to decorate any room in the house: hunting scenes, animals, and nautical themes are equally at home in den, bedroom, or family room; spices, vegetables and fruits, or colonial prints add bright touches to the bath, kitchen, or laundry room.

Materials: One tea towel with the design of your choice, backing material cut slightly larger than the tea towel (no exact measurements are given here, for tea towels vary in size and shape; any backing material will have to be cut to match what you have), quilting or heavy-duty thread, quilting needle, dacron batt cut to the same size as the backing material, 1 package of curtain weights, two ½" wooden dowels or curtain rods with decorative finials (lengths determined by width of tea towel, plus at least 3" for dowel or rod), thread to match the background color of the tea towel.

1. Place tea towel face *up* on a flat surface. Lay backing face *down* over the tea towel, then place batting on top of the backing material. Pin all three layers together (illustration 1).

2. Turn piece over so that the batting is on the bottom and the wrong side of tea towel is facing you.

3. Sew around three sides and part of the fourth leaving openings at the corners to pass the curtain rods or dowels through (illustration 2). Trim corners and turn to the right side, with batting between.

4. Place curtain weights inside the hanging along the bottom edge and tack them in place. Run dowels or curtain rods inside along the bottom and top edges (illustration 3). If openings are too large, close them by stitching until the rod is snugly held. Tack the dowels into place and close opening in fourth side.

5. Begin to quilt around the motifs and design on the tea towel; be as detailed or as general as you wish, but try to make stitches even and well-spaced over the face of the hanging. This will keep the batting in place.

6. Crochet or braid yarn into a cord to hang the towel. Yarn tassels are optional. (Directions for making tassels are on page 53.) A suggestion: why not make quilted pictures from the large illustrations printed on curtain fabrics?

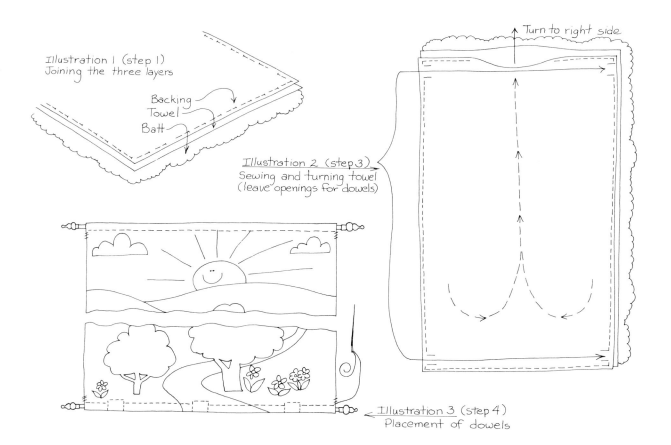

Illustration 1 (step 1)
Joining the three layers

Backing
Towel
Batt

Illustration 2 (step 3)
Sewing and turning towel
(leave openings for dowels)

Turn to right side

Illustration 3 (step 4)
Placement of dowels

Azteca Room Divider

(For color photo see page 52)

Two Central American Indian art forms combine to create our room divider, bringing some of the color and spirit of these nations into your home. The technique of layering colors comes from the San Blas Islands near Panama, while the design influence is found in the incised coin and wall decorations of the ancient Aztecs. Modular in its concept, the divider is reversible and may be hung in several combinations. It measures approximately 4½' x 7'.

Materials: 2½ yards of yellow felt, 2½ yards of green felt, ½ yard of orange felt, thread to match all three colors, and one ¾" wide, 6' long wooden dowel.

1. Cut two ½' x 7½' green felt strips for narrow banners, one 1½' x 7½' strip for wide banner and one 1' x 7½' strip for medium banner from yellow felt.
2. Enlarge patterns to proper size. Trace onto cardboard and mark with numbers and colors.
3. Arrange patterns on proper strips according to overall diagram and trace onto felt with a marking pen.
4. Using sharp scissors, cut the patterns out of the strips, leaving the edges of the holes smooth (illustration 1); cuticle scissors with curved blades are good for cutting curved pieces. The *strips* with cutout areas

form the first "layer" of the applique. Save the cutouts.

5. Now make the cutouts for the second "layer" by laying the cardboard patterns on the proper color of felt and adding about ¼" around all edges of all patterns. Cut out these pieces and place them over corresponding holes in the banners. Position them so that they completely cover the openings (illustration 2).
6. You will notice in the photograph and in the overall diagram that pieces 1a, 7a, 1b, and 7b have holes that are filled by yellow felt. Cut the holes in these pieces and then cut yellow "fillers" from the scraps of yellow felt you saved in step 4 (remember to add ¼" all around for overlap). Place these fillers over corresponding holes (illustration 3).
7. Pin everything in place and turn the banners over to the cut sides. Sew the yellow fillers into place first, working from the cut side, then sew remaining pieces into place (illustration 4). Try not to stitch entirely through the cutouts; this will make the banners reversible. (For applique stitches, see page 23.)
8. When finished, turn over 1" on the top edges of the banners to the sides which have layers of felt pieces. Pin down and stitch turned edges (illustration 5) to form channels. Pass dowel through channels and hang banners.

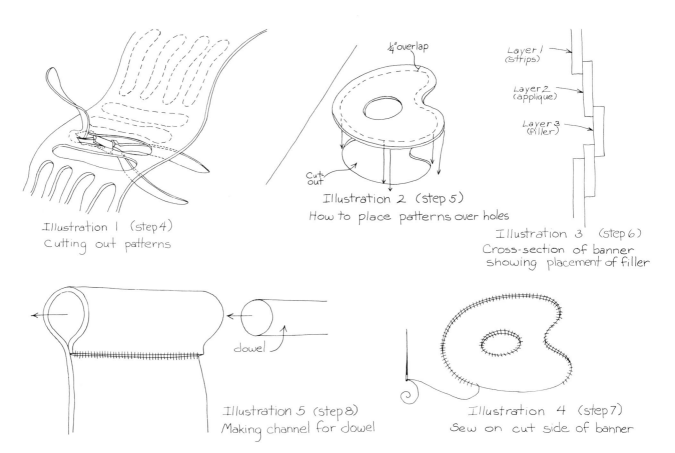

Illustration 1 (step 4)
Cutting out patterns

Illustration 2 (step 5)
How to place patterns over holes

Illustration 3 (step 6)
Cross-section of banner
showing placement of filler

Illustration 5 (step 8)
Making channel for dowel

Illustration 4 (step 7)
Sew on cut side of banner

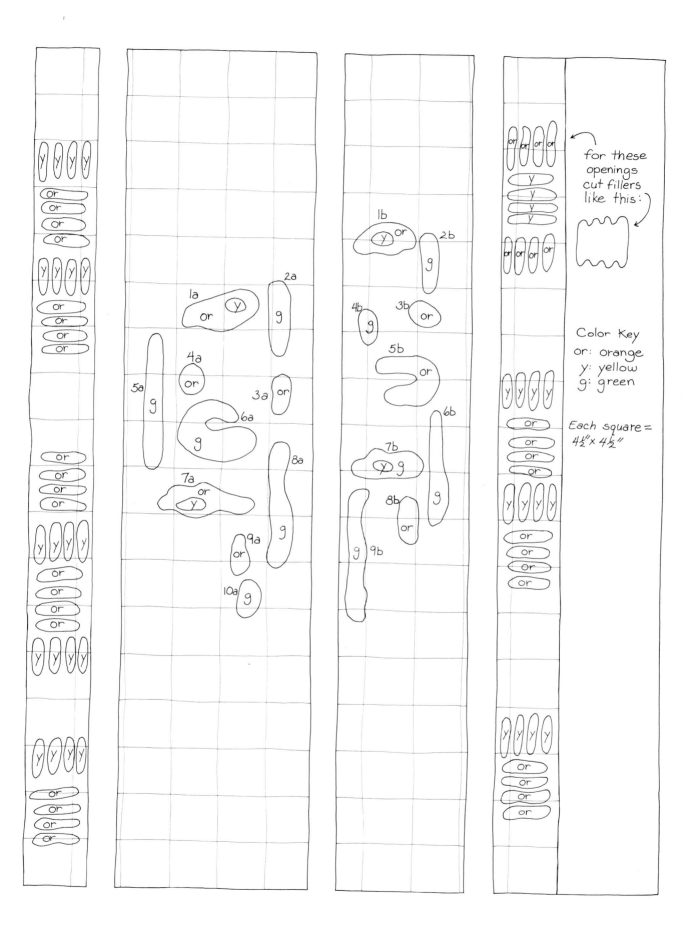

for these openings cut fillers like this:

Color Key
or: orange
y: yellow
g: green

Each square = 4½" x 4½"

HOW TO CREATE AN UNUSUAL QUILT

There's more than one way to create a quilt. Here are eighteen capsule ideas for creating quilted or patchworked objects using a variety of techniques. These are only simplified explanations; it would take an entire book to cover all methods fully. More detailed reading on each method may be found in your local library, and adult education or high school and college extension courses may teach these techniques.

Some methods are more complicated than others, but all are well within the means of the average person. Most equipment may be found in art supply centers, stationery stores, notion shops, the neighborhood grocery store, and your own kitchen.

These techniques have been divided into three basic groupings: freehand applications, printed applications, and needlecraft applications. Some of the ideas and equipment are shown on the facing page.

Printed Applications

The following methods use a block, or carrier, when transferring designs.

Block Printing. Designs are traced onto linoleum blocks, then borders are cut away to form a pattern on the surface of the block. The design is inked, then fabric is carefully laid over the design and a brayer is rolled over the fabric, transferring the design to the cloth surface.

Monoprinting. Textile inks or dyes are used to paint a design onto a sheet of glass. Fabric is then laid over the glass and brayer is rolled over the fabric, transferring the pattern from the glass to the cloth. Only one print may be pulled from a monoprint.

Potato Printing. Cut a baking potato in half and incise a design on the white area. Cut away unwanted parts to make a design in relief. Blot potato to remove juices then dip design into fabric dye and print onto your cloth in single or repeat patterns. When images dry, iron to make them permanent.

Silk Screening. Designs are cut into a lacquer film, exposed onto photosensitized film, or painted with glue to form a mask, then adhered to a screen made of silk stretched like a canvas. The fabric is placed beneath the flat side of the screen and ink is passed through the open areas of the screen/mask onto the fabric.

Transfer Art. A new process has been developed for lifting images from the printed page and transferring them to fabric with no loss in brilliance or color. Kits may be found in hobby and art supply stores.

Freehand Applications

These techniques use random methods of design creation, allowing for variation in the image.

Batik. This is a method of decorating fabric by painting certain areas with wax then dyeing them. The wax resists the dye, leaving coated areas undyed. Many colors may be applied in this manner by reapplying the wax, then dyeing again and again to achieve a multicolor effect. The wax is removed by ironing.

Marbling. In this process, oil base inks suspended in a *size* made from water boiled with moss or cornstarch are manipulated into random patterns; fabric is then laid over the design and saturated, setting the oil base ink design into the cloth. When dry, iron the colored areas to make them permanent.

Painting. Textile dyes may be thinned with water and used to paint a design onto a block or the entire surface of your piece. Pencil in the outlines, then paint as though painting a canvas with watercolors. Oil base embroidery paints are useful for fine lines. When dry, iron the painted areas thoroughly to make permanent.

Tie and Dye. Fabric is folded, twisted, knotted, or tied in certain areas with rubber bands or clamped with pieces of wood cut into designs to create random patterns. It is then dipped into fabric dye. The cloth is dried, and rubber bands or blocks removed to reveal the finished design.

Waterproof Markers. Laundry markers and waterproof fine line marking pens make ideal tools for line drawings on fabric. They won't bleed or rub off, and they come in a good range of colors.

Needlecraft Applications

Surfaces are transformed by the addition of needlecraft embellishments.

Collage. Usually a technique applied to paper, this method adapts well to cloth and related materials. Combine felt, beads, sequins, ribbon, rickrack, trim, braid, lace, and other items to make a special gift item. (Like most special creations, this should be drycleaned.)

Embroidery. Blocks with preprinted embroidery patterns may be purchased or you may create your own designs. Best worked in block form, embroidery can range from airy, decorative flowers and vines to solid pictorial embroidery, such as crewel and satin-type stitches.

Freehand Machine Stitching. Place fabric in an embroidery hoop, lower the feed dogs on your sewing machine, adjust the thread tension, and you're ready to do freehand stitching to create all sorts of individual designs.

Lettering. Letters can be cut from felt or other materials and appliqued, or quilted, printed, drawn or painted on your piece. Make an alphabet quilt or personalize your work by adding the name of the recipient and the occasion.

Quilted Pictures. Drapery or upholstery fabrics, the modern Finnish fabrics, and any fabric with a large bold design or a scene from nature or the city make interesting pictures. Add backing and a batt, then quilt around the shapes. When finished, frame and hang the picture.

Ribbon Applique. Basketweave ribbons over a colored or white background to make an unusual quilt or pillow top. The ribbons are pinned in place, then sewn down. They may then be quilted or left as they are for a pretty effect.

Tablecloth Quilt. A large sized tablecloth of cotton or any other suitable material containing a design you find pleasing may be used as a quilt top and quilted into a comforter or throw.

Yo-yo Quilt or Throw. Cut 3-inch circles from fabric scraps, stitch around the edges, gather, then press each one flat and tie the threads to hold in place. Sew these circlets to one another to make an unusual quilt top. Add backing to make the throw more functional.

Related tools *used for printing patterns onto fabric with three different methods are shown above. Clockwise from left they are block, mono, and potato printing.*

Images *may be drawn, painted, or transferred onto cloth using indelible markers, textile paints, or a solution for transferring the ink from paper to fabric (right).*

Related needlecrafts *give your project punch and an individual look. Collage different materials together (upper left), basket weave ribbons into a field of color (upper right), cut letters from felt or cotton and applique them to your work (lower left), or embroider individual blocks (lower right). Other needlecraft techniques are described on facing page.*

Roman Stripe Patchwork Quilt

A briliant mélange of cotton scraps, this quilt has a Roman Carnival gaiety, hence its name: Roman Stripe. Seemingly intricate, it is the most simple of designs, relying only on the alternation of horizontally striped blocks with vertically striped blocks for this effect.

Here are the measurements for making the Roman Stripe Quilt in the following sizes: twin size: 72" x 100" using 936 blocks (26 blocks x 36 blocks); double size: 81" x 100" using 1,080 blocks (30 blocks x 36 blocks); and king size: 92" x 112" using 1,320 blocks (33 blocks x 40 blocks). If the prospect of putting together so many blocks daunts your spirit, how about enlarging the blocks? To enlarge, use the figures in parentheses as you follow instructions. For twin size you'll need 368 blocks; for double size, 414 blocks; and for king size, 567 blocks.

Materials: a large variety of plain and small print cotton scraps (synthetic fabrics may also be used if they approximate cotton), heavy-duty white thread, dacron batt slightly larger than the desired size of the quilt, enough cotton material to make a backing slightly bigger than the finished size of the quilt (see page 11 on estimating yardage), and several packages of 1" cotton bias binding tape for binding the quilt.

1. Make several cardboard patterns measuring 1½" x 3½" (2" x 5"). Try to cut them as accurately as possible; this will greatly help in constructing the quilt.

2. Begin to trace and cut out pattern pieces, making twice as many from plain fabric as from printed fabric. When constructing a block, a print strip is placed between two plain strips to emphasize the print and to give the quilt some continuity.

3. Taking ¼" seam allowance, begin to sew strips together to form blocks, keeping the center strips about 1" (1½") in width. Three strips, two plain and one printed, make up 1 block measuring 3½" x 3½" (5" x 5"). Watching color placement, continue to construct blocks until you have the correct number.

4. Gather up all of the blocks and lay them out on top of the bed that they will eventually cover. (If this is not possible, use the floor or any flat surface.) Being sure to have the correct number across and down the bed, begin to shuffle the blocks around until colors and patterns are evenly distributed. For an idea of the general appearance, take a look at the color photo (opposite). Notice how colors and prints are spread out evenly to avoid drawing the eye to any one spot.

5. When blocks are placed to your satisfaction, carefully stack the blocks in order, moving from left to right

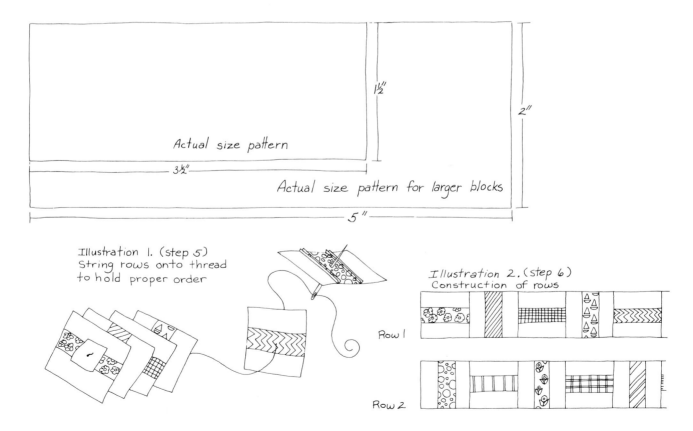

1½"

2"

Actual size pattern

3½"

Actual size pattern for larger blocks

5"

Illustration I. (step 5)
String rows onto thread
to hold proper order

Illustration 2. (step 6)
Construction of rows

Row 1

Row 2

Seemingly a maze *of involved color placement and tone, the secret of the Roman Stripe lies in a simple method of construction.*

and starting a new stack for each row. String them onto a length of thread to keep them together properly. Include a label indicating which row the stack of blocks is from (illustration 1).

6. Take the first row and begin to sew the blocks together, placing the stripe of the blocks alternately horizontally and vertically. After finishing the first row, go on to the next, being sure to alternate the blocks in this row the opposite from the blocks in the first row. Example: begin row 1 with a block striped horizontally, then add the second block in a vertically striped position. Continue until the row is completed. Start row 2 with a block striped vertically, then add a second block

in horizontal stripes. Continue until row is finished (illustration 2). When completed, label according to row.

7. When all rows are completed, join them in proper order to complete the top. Match corners of blocks carefully (see page 15 for this method). Press all seams flat and to one side.

8. Sew together the lengths of cotton to make the backing. Then add the dacron batting and either set the quilt into a quilting frame and quilt by hand (see page 26) or baste all layers and quilt by machine. (Tightly roll the quilt halfway to fit it under the sewing arm.) To bind the quilt, use 1″ cotton bias binding tape (see page 31 for methods of binding).

Sunbonnet Sue Applique Quilt

Would you like to make some very special friends for your child? Just sew up this quilt full of lively little people for your youngster's bed. Sunbonnet Sue and Overall Bill have been "best friends" with several generations of children. Perhaps your little one would enjoy knowing them.

Here are the measurements for making this quilt in the following sizes: twin size: 72" x 100" using 18 blocks, 3 across and 6 down; double size: 81" x 100" using 24 blocks, 4 across and 6 down; king size: 92" x 112" using 35 blocks, 5 across and 7 down. Each block measures 12" x 16" in its finished size.

Materials: for blocks — 45" wide white cotton or synthetic blend, 2 yards for twin size, 2⅔ yards for double size, 4 yards for king size; for backing — 45" wide print of heavyweight cotton, 6 yards for twin size, 6 yards for double size, and 7 yards for king size; for border — 3 yards of 45" wide yellow cotton or synthetic blend; assorted fabric scraps in solid colors or small prints for figures; thread in colors to match or contrast with scraps; white and yellow heavy duty thread; and enough batting for the size quilt you will make.

Add ¼ " seam allowance to blocks and 1" to patterns.

1. Cut out the correct number of blocks for the size you will be making from white fabric.

2. Enlarge patterns to correct size, trace onto tissue paper, and cut them out.

3. You will need 9 girls and 9 boys for the twin size, 12 girls and 12 boys for the double size, and 18 girls and 18 boys for the king size.

4. Draw the pattern pieces on the scraps, adding seam allowances, cut out, and pin the pieces to the block they will occupy. (Example: pin a bonnet and dress to one block and a straw hat, shirt, and overalls to another block.) When all blocks are filled, begin to applique Sue and Bill into place.

5. For Sue: place the dress on the white block where you'd like it to be, pin it into place, and lay a sheet of typing paper beneath the block. With the finest zig-zag stitch on your machine, applique the dress to the block, sewing along pencil line and through the typing paper. Pin the sunbonnet into place and sew it down. When finished, tear away the typing paper from the back and clip away excess fabric around the applique.

6. For Bill: follow the same steps as outlined in step 5 but begin with the shirt, then sew the overalls down and add the straw hat last.

7. These appliques may also be done by hand. Trace

Each square = 2¼" x 2¼"

Each square = 2¼" x 2¼"

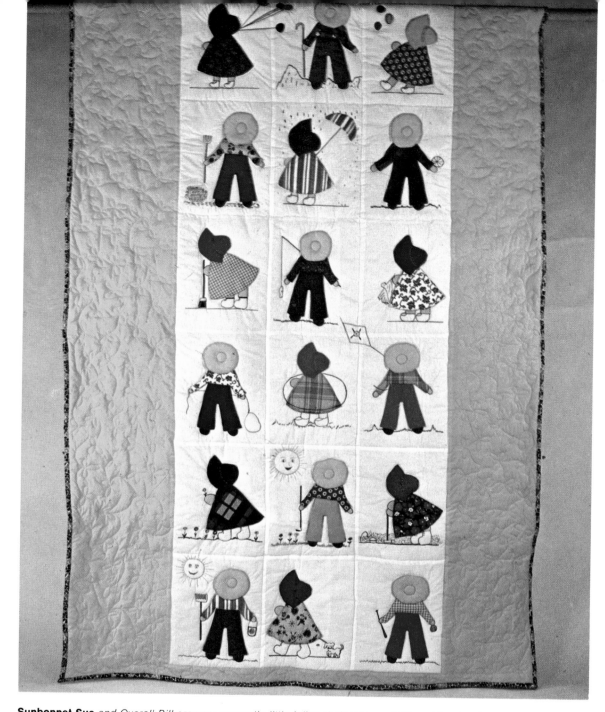

Sunbonnet Sue *and Overall Bill are very energetic little folks; their many activities will entertain your youngster.*

and cut out the patterns, adding ¼" for seam allowance, clip edges and turn under, then baste into place. Pieces may then be attached with applique stitches or decorative embroidery stitches.

8. Hands, feet, and activities may be lightly penciled in and done either with embroidery or drawn in, using oil-base embroidery paints sold in tubes at most needlework or department stores.

9. When all blocks are completed, join them into rows, alternating Sue and Bill (see color photo, above). Be sure to match corners of blocks properly.

10. Sew blocks into rows and then sew the rows into one complete piece. Press seams flat to one side.

11. To make the border, split the 3 yards of yellow fabric down the fold and sew one to each long side of the joined blocks. Use leftover width of material to make 3" borders on top and bottom of joined blocks.

12. To make the backing, divide the backing fabric crosswise into 2 lengths, then, right sides facing, sew together on one side and press the seam open.

13. Lay backing on its face and place batt, then top (right side up) over it. Pin layers together and quilt along the seams of the blocks and around each figure. Any type of quilting pattern relating to the central design may be used to quilt the yellow border area.

14. Bind with backing and miter corners (page 31).

Baby Quilt

(For color photo see page 66)

A crib quilt for the new baby makes a perfect shower or christening gift. Ours is made of softest tricot, downy dacron batt, and gentle cotton lace. Hand-washable, the quilt is also reversible, going from jonquil yellow to pale mint green. Make up your own color combination in pastel or white satin, tricot, cotton-dacron blend, or whipped cream crepe. Plain fabric is best for this coverlet; the most important decoration is the quilting itself. Finished quilt measures about 60″ x 42″.

Materials: A 63″ long x 45″ wide piece of each: yellow tricot, mint green tricot, and dacron batt; white thread, and 6 yards of gathered cotton lace.

1. Enlarge quilting pattern to correct size from the diagram on the facing page.
2. Trace pattern onto newsprint or butcher paper and draw over the design with a heavy black line, using a felt tip marking pen. Allow to dry thoroughly.
3. Lay the yellow tricot over the pattern face up and tape it into place. You will be able to see the lines of the design faintly through the tricot. Trace over the pattern with a medium soft lead pencil to transfer the design to the tricot (illustration 1). For other methods of transferring patterns, refer to page 26.

4. Place mint green tricot face *down* on a flat surface, lay batting over green tricot, then put yellow tricot face *up* over batting. Pin all layers together along the basting lines as shown on page 26.
5. Place quilt onto the frame (page 26) or quilt off the frame (see pages 26-27 for instructions on quilting).
6. When quilting is finished, remove from the frame and take out all pins.
7. Trim batting to match edges of tricot. Push batting back, turn under the edges of the yellow tricot (illustration 2), and pin.
8. Pin cotton lace along the edges of the green tricot and machine stitch (illustration 3).
9. Turn seam to inside and pin turned edge of yellow tricot over the lace (illustration 4). Sew yellow tricot edge to lace with an invisible stitch (for an illustration of stitch, see page 23).

A suggestion: if you don't care for cotton lace trim on the baby quilt, how about a satin binding? Satin blanket bias edging can be found in department stores, sewing centers, notion shops, and dime stores. For directions on how to attach, see pages 31-32 on finishing and binding. Those pages contain a variety of methods that may be used to bind your baby quilt: lace, braid, rickrack, or self binding.

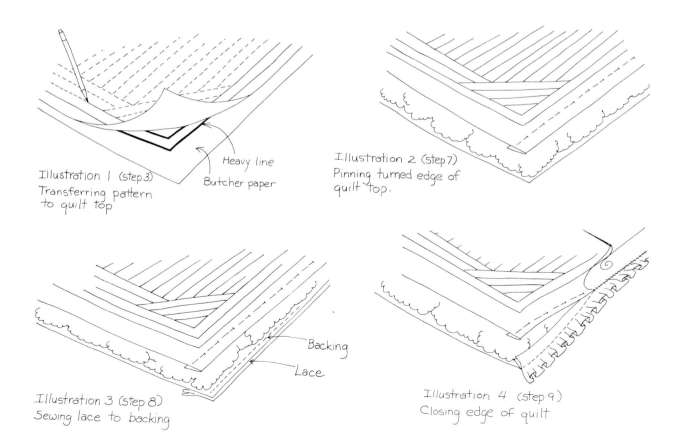

Illustration 1 (step 3)
Transferring pattern to quilt top

Heavy line
Butcher paper

Illustration 2 (step 7)
Pinning turned edge of quilt top.

Illustration 3 (step 8)
Sewing lace to backing

Backing
Lace

Illustration 4 (step 9)
Closing edge of quilt

Each mark equals 1"

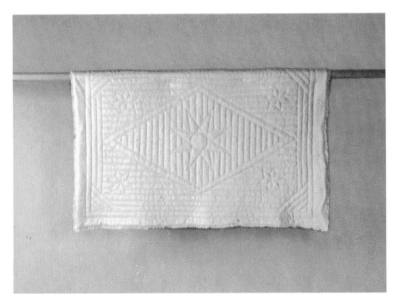

Soft, downy baby's quilt *is made of gentle tricot and edged with cotton lace. Light yellow is a cheerful color for baby's first crib quilt.*

Uncannily *like a lovely coastal landscape, this crazy patch quilt has the distinct feel of rolling land, vegetation, and salt sea air. Embroidery adds a delicate floral touch.*

Landscape Crazy Patch Quilt

(For color photo see facing page)

Pretend you're a bird flying over a seaboard landscape. When you look down, what do you see? Water, waves, sand, hills, trees, farms, valleys, streams? Now look on the facing page and you'll see these things in our Landscape Crazy Patch Quilt. It takes a little imagination, but you can almost find little homes dotting the landscape and livestock grazing in seaside pastures. The unusual mood of this quilt comes from the integration of greens, blues, and subtle earth tones lightly traced with floral embroidery. Finished size is 75″ x 75″. For more information on crazy patch quilts, see page 18.

Materials: wool scraps of green, blue, and earth tones cut into medium large random shapes (wash wool to preshrink and ensure colorfastness before cutting; see photo on facing page for pattern shapes), 4¼ yards 45″ wide green flannel for backing, 4½ yards muslin, green yarn for ties, embroidery floss, and dacron batt.

1. Cut muslin into 16 blocks, each 20″ x 20″. Lay wool scraps on blocks to cover entirely and arrange into designs similar to those shown in color photograph. Edges of scraps should overlap slightly. When you are satisfied, pin pieces in place.

2. Press overlapping edges under and baste down. Hand sew each scrap with an invisible stitch (see page 23) until all turned edges except outside edges have been sewn down. Complete remainder of blocks.

3. Decorative embroidery stitches emphasize certain areas and add visual interest. A sampling of these stitches may be seen below. Embroidered flowers and birds are added to scraps larger than 5 inches.

4. When all blocks have been completed and embroidered, join by first pinning them into rows and sewing with a ⅝″ seam, then by joining rows. When joining rows, match corners and seams carefully by pinning through each set of matching seams (see page 15). When all blocks are sewn together, embroider over the seams formed where the blocks join.

5. Cut flannel in half crosswise and sew together along one longer edge to form a piece 76½″ x 89″.

6. Place crazy patch top face down on a flat surface, lay 76″ x 80″ rectangle of batting over the top, then place flannel backing right side up over the batt. Pin thoroughly with safety pins.

7. Following directions for tying a quilt found on page 28, make yarn ties on the flannel backing corresponding to the centers and corners of the squares on the top. Catch only the muslin lining so that no ties show on front.

8. Turn in all edges; sew with invisible stitch.

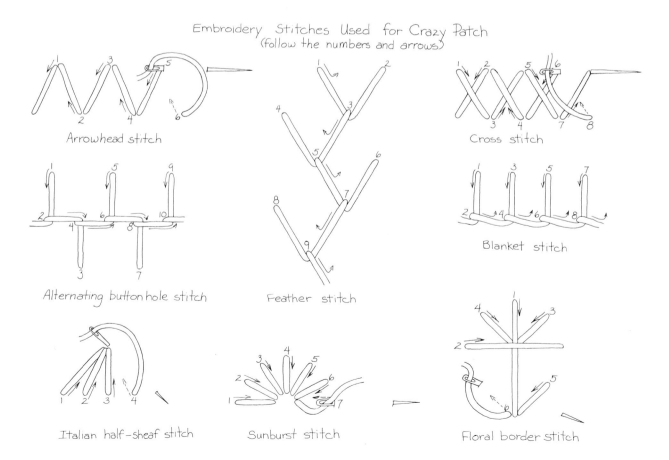

Embroidery Stitches Used for Crazy Patch
(follow the numbers and arrows)

Arrowhead stitch

Cross stitch

Alternating button hole stitch

Feather stitch

Blanket stitch

Italian half-sheaf stitch

Sunburst stitch

Floral border stitch

Optical art *with a touch of nostalgia, our Grandmother's Flower Garden Quilt abstracts the lovely Victorian garden of yesterday into a pastel geometric statement in fabric.*

Lush tropical vegetation *and soft trade winds are fondly captured in this Hawaiian Quilt called "Kamakani Kaili Aloha"— the wind that wafts love from one to another.*

Grandmother's Flower Garden Quilt

(For color photo see facing page)

Sunny and gay, Grandmother's Flower Garden invites you to slip back to the gardens of yesteryear for a leisurely stroll. Enclosed by yellow pathways, fat sunbursts of flowers range from deep hues to shady pastels, creating a quilt especially appropriate for any sunny room. This quilt may be made in three sizes: twin size, 72" x 100"; double size, 81" x 100"; or king size, 92" x 112". Twin size contains 72 flowers, 8 across and 9 down; double size has 90 flowers, 9 across and 10 down; and king size contains 110 flowers, 10 across and 11 down.

Materials: a large amount of scraps in cotton or synthetic blends — plain fabrics and small print fabrics are best (¼ yard of 45" wide fabric makes 48 hexagons), 3 yards of 45" wide yellow fabric for pathways, dacron batt large enough to fit the quilt, enough 45" wide yellow fabric for a backing the same size as the quilt, and yellow heavy duty thread.

1. Following directions on page 20, make several cardboard patterns for a hexagon 2½" in diameter (after many tracings cardboard wears down, so you'll need several fresh patterns).
2. For each flower you will need: 1 yellow hexagon for the center of the flower, 6 plain hexagons for the first ring of petals, and 12 print hexagons for the second ring of petals. Place flower groups in envelopes or clip them together to prevent loss.
3. When you have enough flowers for your quilt, arrange them in rows, according to color photo, keeping colors evenly placed. You will notice that flowers run in rows on the horizontal and diagonal only. Vertically they run in zigzag fashion.
4. When colors are arranged satisfactorily, begin to cut out yellow hexagons for pathways. When all pieces are cut, arrange flowers and pathways in proper order in horizontal offset rows. (For set of design, see illustration 1, below).
5. Sew hexagons together in strips running horizontally (illustration 2). Sew hexagons together until all are sewn into strips in their correct order.
6. Then sew row one to row two, moving the rows back and forth in a zigzag motion to maneuver them under the sewing machine needle (illustration 3). Sew all rows together. Press seams out from centers of flowers to make quilting easier.
7. Lay top over backing and batt, baste, then quilt, using pattern shown below (illustration 4).
8. Bind by turning edges in and sew with invisible stitch (see page 23 for stitch diagram).

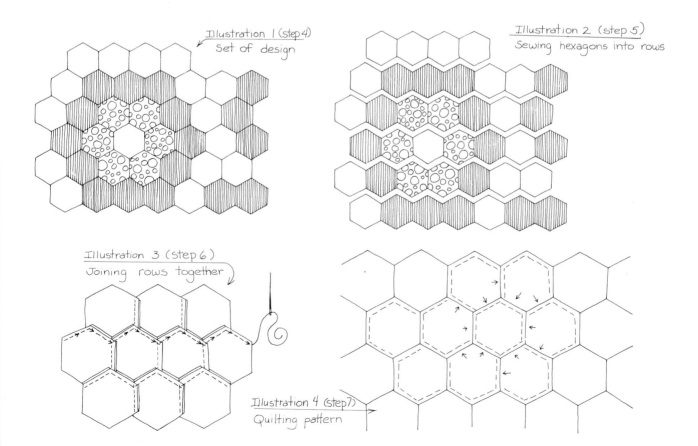

Illustration 1 (step 4)
Set of design

Illustration 2 (step 5)
Sewing hexagons into rows

Illustration 3 (step 6)
Joining rows together

Illustration 4 (step 7)
Quilting pattern

Wafting Winds Hawaiian Quilt

(For color photo see page 68)

The legendary beauty of Hawaiian quilts is personified in the dense greenery of this example called Kamakani Kaili Aloha—in translation, "the wind that wafts love from one to another." Graceful flowing lines combine with sharp frondlike points reminiscent of palms and tropical flowers, creating a unique and intricate applique design in kelly green on a white background.

Because of its complexity of design, the Hawaiian quilt is not recommended as a beginning project. Save this one for later, for a great deal of time and work is required. This quilt, pictured on page 68, took two years to make, but the results clearly indicate that every stitch was well worth the effort. If you like the idea, try it out in cushion size first to see if you want to take it further.

Hawaiian quilts are usually made in three sizes: twin size: 84" x 108"; double size: 99" x 108"; and king size: 108" x 108". Vary the distance between border and center design to fit your quilt.

Materials: for twin size, 7 yards; for double size, 8 yards; for king size, 9 yards *each* 45" wide plain yardage for backing, colored yardage for applique, and plain yardage for quilt top; 1 dacron batt in the proper size; white basting thread, 2 to 4 spools of quilting thread, and 2 spools thread to match applique.

1. Preshrink fabrics before using and iron out creases.
2. As shown in illustration 1, fold a piece of 8½" x 11" typing paper and draw your design along the tapered edges of the triangle. Cut out, being careful not to cut through the edges, then unfold the design. Do this until you get a design you like. A border design may be planned, using the rectangle of paper left over.
3. Cut yardage for quilt top into 3 equal lengths crosswise and sew together along selvages with a ½" seam to make one large piece (illustration 2). Do the same for applique fabric and for backing.
4. Fold applique fabric into a triangle as shown in illustration 3. Cut a triangle of the same size from butcher paper and transfer your applique design to the triangle. Only ⅛ of the design, a pie-shaped wedge, is drawn on the triangle. It will look similar to illustration 1 but will be only one thickness.
5. Lay pattern over folded applique material, match center points, pin into place, and cut around pattern through all eight layers.
6. Unfold the applique and lay it out over the quilt top, matching seams of applique to seams of quilt top. When laid out to your satisfaction, baste pattern into place, securing points first. Baste ½" in from cut edges, leaving enough fabric to turn under.

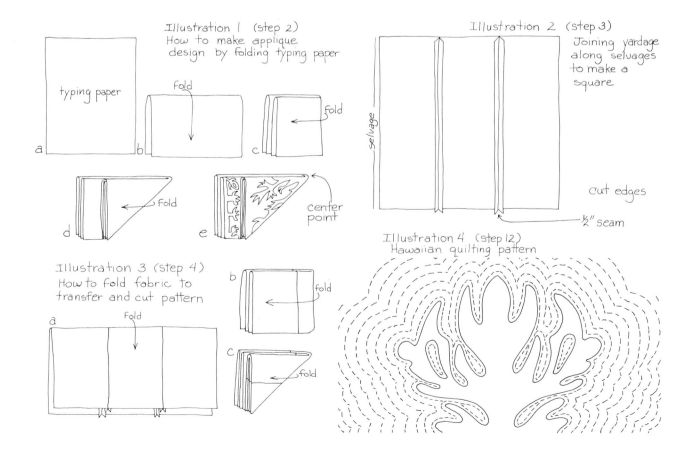

Illustration 1 (step 2)
How to make applique design by folding typing paper

typing paper
fold
fold
Fold
center point

Illustration 3 (step 4)
How to fold fabric to transfer and cut pattern
Fold
fold
fold

Illustration 2 (step 3)
Joining yardage along selvages to make a square
selvage
cut edges
½" seam

Illustration 4 (step 12)
Hawaiian quilting pattern

Diagram equals ⅛ of total applique pattern. Border pattern runs along bottom. For king size, each square equals 4¼" x 4¼". For double size each square equals 7½" x 7½"; add 5½" to width of top and bottom borders to make central design square. For twin size each square equals 6⅓" x 6⅓"; add 12" to width of top and bottom borders to make central design square.

7. Enlarge your border design and cut it from fabric left over from cutting central design.

8. Begin to applique central design by clipping curves slightly and turning under edges as you go. Sew with an invisible stitch to secure applique to quilt top, using thread in a matching color.

9. When center is appliqued, add border design to top and pin into place. Baste from corners in toward centers of sides, then applique to quilt top.

10. Remove all basting stitches and pins when finished with applique work.

11. Following the directions on page 25, construct a quilting frame. When ready, put backing into frame,

then lay dacron batt over the backing. Place appliqued quilt top over batt and center. When in place, baste all three layers together securely.

12. Hawaiian quilting patterns aren't drawn onto the quilt top. Just follow the outlines of the applique in a ripple effect going out from the center (illustration 4), keeping quilting lines ¼" to ½" apart.

13. When quilting is finished, edges may be bound with bias tape, with the back, or with the top of the quilt itself. Information on binding may be found on page 31. A suggestion: try making up your own Hawaiian quilt pattern. It's like cutting out paper snowflakes, but thinking in terms of vegetation.

Log Cabin/Checkerboard Quilt

(For color photo see page 34)

Our Log Cabin throw has more to it than good looks. On the reverse side it becomes a portable checkerboard, complete with felt checkers. Use it at the beach, in the car, on the living room floor, or anywhere that a game seems in order. A small snap-closed pocket holds the checkers. (The throw measures 4' x 6'.)

Materials: 4½ yards 36" wide muslin; 4¼ yards 45" wide blue denimlike slubbed material; ½ yard 45" wide fabric each: blue print cotton a1 (see illustration 3), blue print cotton a2, red print cotton a3; ¼ yard 45" wide fabric each: red print cotton a4, yellow print cotton a5, yellow print cotton a6, green print cotton a7, white cotton with print; ¼ yard 45" wide fabric in red print cotton, 4' x 6' dacron batt, blue heavy duty thread, and heavy embroidery floss for ties.

1. Wash muslin to shrink it, then cut twenty-four 12½" x 12½" muslin squares.
2. From 1¾ yards of blue denimlike fabric, cut 24 pieces of *each* of the numbered strips as shown below in illustration 1.
3. From *each* of the printed cotton fabrics, cut 24 strips as shown in illustration 2.
This log cabin pattern is made by covering a muslin square with different colored cotton strips, half of which

are plain and half of which are print. When the block is finished, there will be a diagonal division between print and plain.

4. Enlarge diagram A to its correct size and mark all lines with a black marking pen. Lay muslin squares over pattern and transfer lines to muslin with a pencil.
5. Take 1 white print cotton square and sew on four sides to center of muslin (see illustration 3).
6. Lay a8 over center square, right sides facing. Line up raw seams as shown in illustration 3 and sew a8 into place; fold to right side. Attach b8 in the same way, then a7, b7, a6, b6, a5, b5, a4, b4, a3, b3, a2, b2, a1, and b1. Construct 24 squares in this manner. Press all blocks, then lay them face down and mark seam lines on muslin with a pencil.
7. Following diagram B on facing page for placement, sew blocks into rows and rows into completed top, carefully matching all corners.
8. Cut twenty 12½" x 12½" blocks and thirty-two 3½" x 3½" squares from blue denimlike cloth. Cut thirty-two 3½" x 3½" squares from ½ yard of 45" wide fabric in red print.
9. Alternating colors, sew eight 3½" blocks into a row. Make 8 rows and then join the rows as shown in diagram C, making one large checkerboard pattern.
10. Make four rows of 12½" blue squares, 4 squares

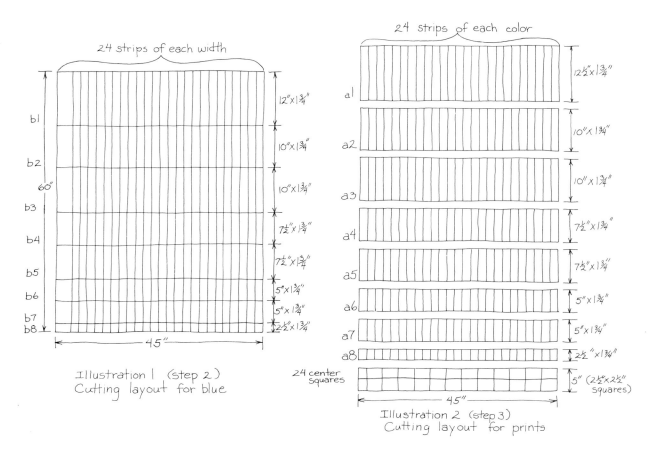

Illustration 1 (step 2)
Cutting layout for blue

Illustration 2 (step 3)
Cutting layout for prints

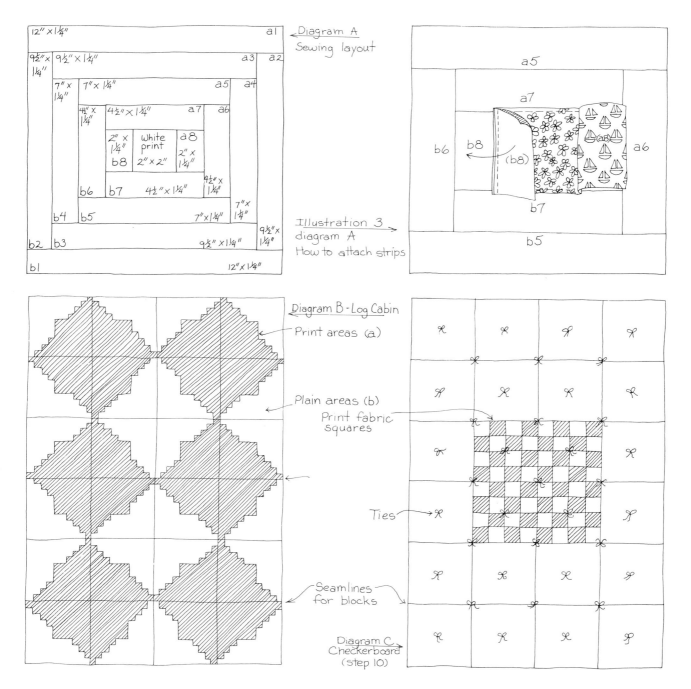

Diagram A
Sewing layout

Illustration 3
diagram A
How to attach strips

Diagram B - Log Cabin
Print areas (a)

Plain areas (b)
Print fabric squares

Ties

Seamlines for blocks

Diagram C
Checkerboard
(step 10)

to a row. Sew remaining 4 squares into pairs, then sew pairs to opposite sides of checkerboard (see diagram C).

11. Join two rows of 12½" squares, and sew them to one open side of checkerboard. Do the same for remaining two rows of 12½" squares (see diagram C).

12. Place log cabin top and checkerboard backing with right sides facing. Matching seam lines of top and back blocks on all edges, pin together and join on three sides and part of the fourth side. Turn throw to right side and press the edges.

13. Insert 4' x 6' rectangle of batting and smooth it into place, carefully filling in the corners.

14. Pin open side of throw together and sew shut with an invisible stitch (for stitch diagram, see page 23).

15. Following instructions on page 28 for tying a quilt, make ties at corners and centers of blocks on checkerboard side using doubled embroidery floss.

16. For optional pocket, cut one rectangle 6½" x 16" from both blue fabric and red print fabric. With right sides facing, join on three sides, then turn. Slipstitch fourth side shut. Fold rectangle to make a 6" deep pocket with a 3" flap and mark folds. Sew back of pocket to corner of throw on checkerboard side. Whip sides of pocket together and add snaps to flap.

17. Make 32 checkers from stuffed 2" felt circles.

A Gallery of Quilts

As techniques, applique, patchwork, and quilting can cross an unlimited number of boundaries to become integral parts of clothing, sculpture, wall hangings, illustrations, and hundreds of other three-dimensional objects. Put these tools in the hands of the artist, and . . .

well, who knows what will evolve in time?

Some exciting applications present themselves on the next few pages to prove that all it takes is a new idea and the tools with which to create. Some are old, some are very new; all are innovative.

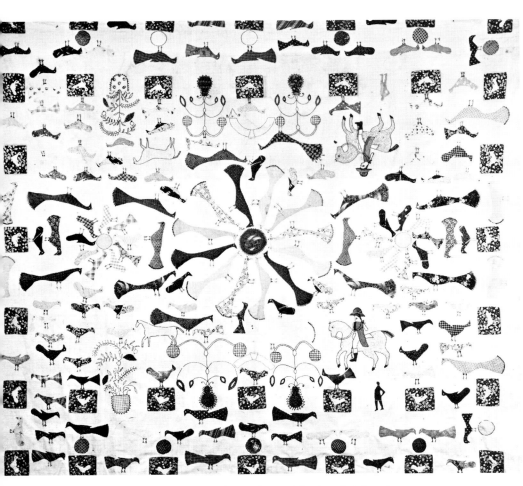

Modern in appearance, *"Peacocks and Peahens" (above) actually came into being during the American Revolution. If you look closely, you will find two "Redcoats" on horseback hiding among the birds. An incredibly fine example of elaborate crazy patchwork may be seen in the dressing gown shown at the right. Fine embroidery edges each patch.*

"Kitchen Quilt" *(above) contains embroidered and appliqued images of foods this cook loves best. Printed fabrics are cleverly used to represent frosting, carrots.*

Batik patchwork *wall hanging (above) uses handprinted fabric to give new twist to traditional patchwork designs. Mounted on a dowel, hanging measures 57½" x 46½".*

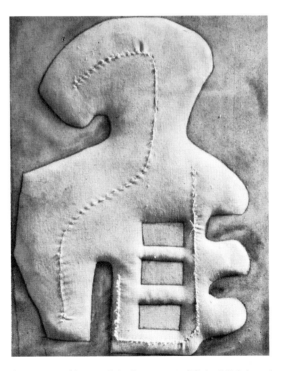

Sutures *and bas-relief effect create "Saboth" (above), a calm, monolithic construction in natural canvas tones. "Peacock Quilt" (left) whimsically clothes this bird in a rainbow of velvet, cotton, satin, and corduroy feathers.*

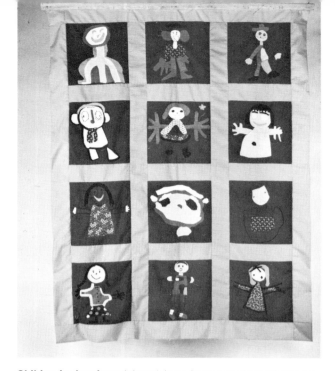

Children's drawings (above) have been transformed into applique blocks to create this personalized quilt.

Mobcapped fairy child dreams sweet dreams on this mint green confection of a quilt (above).

Letters in this alphabet quilt (above) are amusingly illustrated, including a shoe that laces, a zipper that zips.

"Toyland Quilt" (above) contains a host of friendly creatures. Random sizes of the blocks create a relaxed appearance.

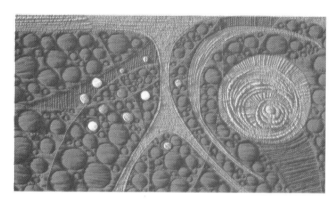

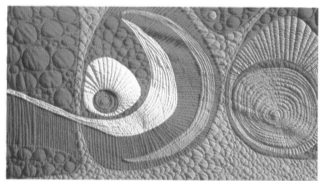

"Favorite Dream with Technicolor Trees" *(details above) is a beautiful example of the finest in applique work and hand quilting applied in a uniquely creative way.*

Fanciful butterfly dress *(above) is richly decorated with hand-painted pastel vines, abstract flowers, and large padded butterflies to create a very individual appearance.*

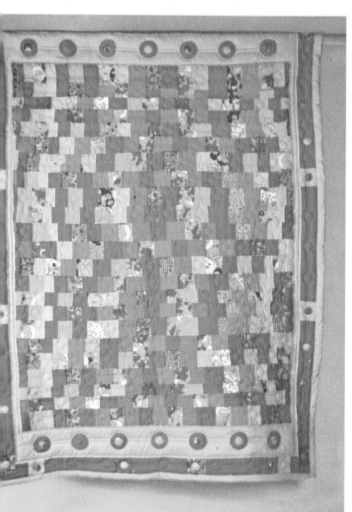

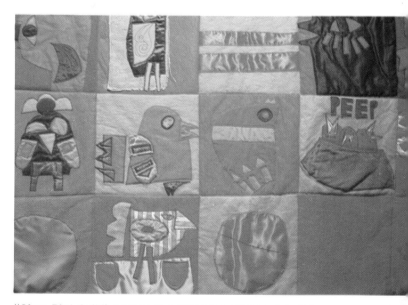

"Giant Bird Quilt" *(above) is a humorous statement in felt, satin, and assorted cottons, all whimsically embellished by cut felt letters, hand and machine stitching.*

A sophisticated study *in red, pink, yellow, and assorted prints, this striking quilt (at left) is appliqued and hand quilted into a geometric palette of moving colors.*

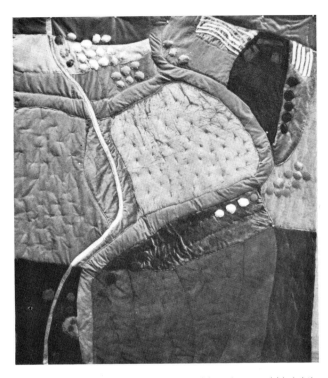

"Farm Landscape Quilt" (above) rambles along amid brightly colored fields, streams, and lots of trees.

A strange, ominous quality pervades "In the Beginning," (above) a 56" x 72" silkscreened, quilted, and stuffed hanging.

"Friendship Quilt" (detail above) contains squares from friends and acquaintances all over the world.

Silver tricot, nylon net, and leather applique are ingeniously combined in "Tularosa Thunderbird" (below).

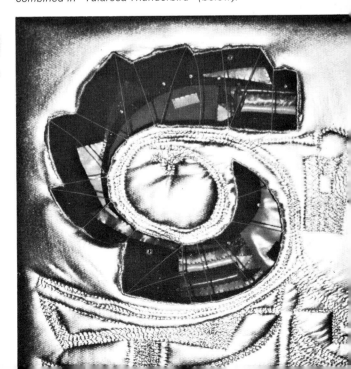

Distinguished by *fine details and intricate stitchery, "Mexican Quilt" (above) is lovingly handmade, a visual travelogue of south-of-the-border memories rendered permanent.*

"In the Beginning" *(above) is an 8 foot long representation of the creation of the world. Patchwork, applique, and stitchery all combine to evoke a feeling of richness.*

"Blue Friendship Quilt" *(above), one of four made over a long weekend, brought friends together and stimulated a burst of creativity and group awareness.*

A beautiful *chronicle of everyday observances, this crazy quilt (at left), made in Vermont in the mid-1800s, includes delightful character studies and animal portraiture in applique.*

Glossary of Terms

Applique. Also called "laid-on" applique, this decoration is formed with pieces cut from one material, arranged into a pattern, then sewn with a hemming stitch onto a background material.

Backing. The bottom layer of the quilt as a whole, or the back of a block or patch. Usually unbleached muslin or cotton sheeting is used, although any cotton fabric in a complementary print or color will do.

Batt. The middle layer, or filling, placed between the top and back of a quilt. It may be cotton or one of the new synthetics, such as dacron. Also called wadding or stuffing.

Binding. The material or process used to finish the edges of a quilt, covering the edges of all layers and holding them together. This is the final step.

Block. For ease in handling and sewing, a quilt is divided into sections (blocks), each a complete pattern. Usually a square, rectangle, or hexagon, a block may be any size containing any number of pieces.

Border. The cloth frame around the patterned central portion of the quilt. The border may be decorated using quilted, patchworked or appliqued designs which complement the overall quilt pattern.

Comforter. A quilt of one color, having top and back of unpieced material quilted in simple or elaborate designs. The name comforter is often used to refer to factory-made, overstuffed quilts of satin or nylon.

Coverlet. A quilt large enough to cover just the top of the bed without hanging over the edges or covering the pillows.

Crazy quilt. A quilt design using irregularly sized and shaped pieces of cloth in different colors and textures, fitted together like a puzzle.

Dividers. Methods used to set together a quilt, using strips of material placed between blocks to create a lattice-work effect, or joining blocks to one another, forming one large quilt top.

English padding. A quilting variation, this technique is used to pad only certain enclosed areas of a quilt, leaving other surfaces flat by stuffing loose batting only into areas outlined by stitches.

Hexagonal patchwork. An optical pattern, this style of pieced quilt is made with six-sided blocks sewn together on all edges. Great care must be taken that corners are sharp and side seams straight.

Marking. The process of drawing the quilting design on the top or back of your piece before starting to quilt.

Mitering. A neat way to turn a 90° corner when binding the edges of a quilt. At the corners, a diagonal seam runs from the inside angle to the outside corner of the binding material.

Patch. An over-exercised word in quilting. The word patch can mean several things: a block; the process of piecing the quilt together; applique.

Patchwork. Designs formed by small pieces of material sewn together, usually in the form of a block. Can also refer to the technique of applique.

Piecework. The process of joining small pieces of material to form an overall design.

Quilt. The finished product, or the process of sewing the layers of a quilt together using small, even stitches in a decorative design.

Rolling a quilt. Literally, to roll the already quilted portion of your quilt onto the frame, making it easier to reach the next area to be quilted.

Setting together. Sewing the completed blocks together to form the intended quilt design. This may be done by several methods: strips, alternating blocks, block to block, or diagonal set.

Template. A pattern made from durable material (such as cardboard or plastic), used to draw pattern pieces onto fabric. This ensures uniformity in size and shape, so that all pieces will fit together precisely.

Throw. An individual-sized coverlet, normally used to cover a napping or resting person.

Tied quilt. The quilt top, filler, and backing are fastened together with yarn knots at regular intervals all over the quilt.

Trapunto. A decorative design of lines stitched ¼ inch apart through two layers of fabric; the channel is then stuffed with yarn to form a relief pattern or outline.

Photo credits: Karen Bakke, 77 lower right; R. R. Dvorak, 78 upper left, Alyson Smith Gonsalves, 4, 5, 7 all, 8, 9 all, 35, 59 all, 61, 63, 66 all, 68 all, 74 lower right, 75 lower left, right, 76 all, 77 upper right, lower left, 79 upper left, right; Bill Haddox, 77 upper left; Joanne Leonard, 79 lower right; Joan Lintault, 75 upper left; Kathryn McCardle, 78 lower left; T. Fred Miller, 78 upper right; E. E. Nichols, 75 upper right; Shelbourne Museum Incorporated, Shelbourne, Vermont, 74 lower left, 79 lower left; Lars Speyer, Cover, 34, 36, 37, 39, 42 all, 44, 45, 47, 50 all; 52 all; Frances S. Turner, 78 lower right.